"To develop this friend... ...p and his team has been a joy.... Skip and I have a lot in common: we are both great lovers of Jesus Christ."
— Joel C. Rosenberg, Best-selling author

"Skip has been a real blessing in our lives... watching what God is doing in Albuquerque is just amazing. I thank God for him."
— Raul Ries, Pastor and Author

"Skip's vision...and [his] ability to execute and carry out the vision with the overall quality of integrity, bring forth great fruit.
— Dr. Ross Rhoads, Pastor,
Chaplin of Billy Graham Ministries

"When I preached for Pastor Skip Heitzig some time ago I was amazed to find 12,000 people in attendance. I knew this tall, lean, cowboy-looking preacher must be something special, and now that I have read his newest book I realize what it is. He is a warm-hearted communicator of the Word of God who faithfully teaches divine truth with a practical application to everyday life. His love for Jesus Christ comes through on almost every page. This is one of the best books I have read, and I heartily recommend it to everyone. You will be inspired!"
— Tim LaHaye, Author/Pastor

"Skip has been a good friend of mine for years... and it's so exciting to see how God has continued to bless this ministry."
— Greg Laurie, Pastor and Author

HOMELAND SECURITY?

PROTECTING YOUR FAITH, FAMILY & FUTURE

SKIP HEITZIG

BRIDGE
LOGOS
FOUNDATION

Alachua, Florida 32615

Bridge-Logos
Alachua, FL 32615 USA

Homeland Security
by Skip Heitzig

Printed in the United States of America.

Library of Congress Catalog Card Number: 2010927091
International Standard Book Number 978-0-88270-735-8

G616.316.N.m1005.35250

ACKNOWLEDGEMENTS

Thanks to all who helped make this book a reality:
Terry Whalin, editor; our Calvary publishing team,
Brian and Rebekah; Brandi Heft, cover design;
Elizabeth Nason, layout; Jeff Lefever, photography;
Chip Lusko and his team at The Connection;
and all the fine folks at Bridge-Logos. You are all
appreciated. It is a pleasure serving the Lord with you.

This book is dedicated to our wonderful church family.
I count it a privilege to be a part of this "home" we call
Calvary of Albuquerque.

CONTENTS

Chapter 1

THREAT LEVEL—RED?

I was watching the election news coverage of the Iowa Caucus. As the network camera filmed a reporter with his microphone, a large crowd gathered in the background. Directly behind the crowd was a huge sign with a single word that said CHANGE. The reporter used the sign as a prop and said, "The word behind me sums up what the nation is looking for; we're looking for change to occur." But what if change happened without your knowing?

If that sounds impossible, here is an illustration of what I mean: In the 1912 elections, Woodrow Wilson was elected president. He went to visit his elderly aunt, whom he hadn't seen in a long time. When he walked into her room, she said, "Well, Woodrow, what have you been doing lately?"

He paused for a moment and said, "Auntie, I've just been elected the president."

In a surprised tone, his auntie said, "Oh? Of what?"

"Of the United States of America," President Wilson said.

At his words, she bristled back, "Oh, don't be silly."

In our day, with twenty-four-hour news, it's hard to imagine that everyone wouldn't have this information. Yet with President Wilson, his own aunt didn't know about his election. In this context, it is cute and innocent, but what if the change involves warfare or a battle? If you are in such an armed conflict and don't know your enemy, the change could be fatal.

A few years later in 1917, Lawrence of Arabia conquered the city of Agaba at the port of the Red Sea over in the Middle East. The Turks, who ran the city at that time, considered the port city of Agaba to be impregnable because they had huge naval guns positioned in the hills behind the city, pointed out toward the port. Any ship that came into the harbor to attack would be annihilated. Other than the water, the rest of the city was surrounded by an inhospitable barren desert. They thought no one would attack them from the desert. To their surprise, Lawrence of Arabia came through the desert with his warring tribes of citizenry. He flanked them on the north side, their blind side, swept past the naval guns, attacked, and defeated the city. The Turks made two mistakes. First, they didn't identify their enemy; and second, they didn't choose the right weapons.

Until a few years ago, no one in the United States was talking about a war on terror and *al Qaida* wasn't even in our vocabulary. Then, everything changed one Tuesday morning in September 2001. A new enemy had surfaced. Now it's common to consider that some people in the world don't like us and even want to destroy us.

The focus of this book is homeland security, but not in the way that you might think. While our country is in danger of terrorist attacks, and we will touch on that in these pages, we have a greater enemy than terrorism. Yes, our "homeland" is under attack—I'm talking about our homes, our families, our children, and our churches. The key for each of these elements is the matter of the soul, because our souls are also under attack. The Apostle Paul in Ephesians 6:12 gave us the battle briefing: "Our struggle is not against flesh and blood, but against the rulers, against the authorities, against the powers of this dark world" (NIV).

Our real enemy, according to Paul, is a host of demonic beings, including the devil himself. When the average person hears any mention of demons or the devil, their usual response is much like that of Woodrow Wilson's aunt: "Oh, don't be silly. That's not real." People tend to downplay the spiritual aspect of life as though it's not the real problem.

Until the attacks on the World Trade Center, the United States didn't have a Department of Homeland Security, yet now there are 200,000 employees in that federal government department. Their charge is to assess and respond to terrorist threats to the public. They've created a color-coded system with different levels of threat from green to red. Red is the most severe, while green is the most mild. Our current threat level in America is at the elevated yellow level, which means we are under a significant terrorist threat. Whether you fly domestic or international, the level rises to the orange level because flights are a more severe threat with a higher risk of terrorism.

What would the level be on our color chart if we were dealing with a spiritual enemy and facing a spiritual battle? I suggest that it would be in the severe zone, especially for some of us. To begin the teaching on this topic, let's turn to 1 Chronicles 12. This may seem to be an odd chapter to start our study. If you glanced through this chapter, you would see a list of names; it reads as an obituary, with difficult names to pronounce. I do not recommend this chapter for bedside reading unless you use it to make you go to sleep quickly.

But this chapter details the names of David's mighty men, and to David every one of these men was important. These men were David's first string for any battle, and they helped him to win against other kingdoms.

I want to highlight several key verses. First, 1 Chronicles 12:1 says: "Now these were the men who came to David at Ziklag while he was still a fugitive from Saul the son of Kish; and they were among the mighty men, helpers in the war." Then skip down to verse 8, which says, "Some Gadites joined David at the stronghold in the wilderness, mighty men of valor, men trained for battle, who could handle shield and spear, whose faces were like the faces of lions, and were as swift as gazelles on the mountains."

Now let's skip to 1 Chronicles 12:23, which says: "Now these were the numbers of the divisions that were equipped for war, and came to David at Hebron to turn over the kingdom of Saul to him, according to the word of the LORD." Then finally, 1 Chronicles 12:30-32 says:

> Of the sons of Ephraim twenty thousand eight hundred, mighty men of valor, famous men throughout their father's house; of the half-tribe of Manasseh eighteen thousand, who were designated by name to come and make David king; of the sons of Isaachar who had understanding of the times, to know what Israel ought to do, their chiefs were two hundred; and all their brethren were at their command.

In my reading, this final verse reached out and grabbed me. When I reach a series of difficult names to pronounce in the Bible, I have a tendency just to skim through them, but when I got to this final verse, it seemed to say, *Uh, wait a*

4

minute, don't you go anywhere. You stay right here and notice me, because there are some lessons here I want you to learn.

I want to camp on this final verse and use it to launch this book about our spiritual battles. What methods do you use to get discernment and direction with conviction? In these aimless times in which we currently live, how can you think clearly and live with faith and peace in the midst of turmoil? I boiled this starting process into three positive commands to use in threatening times. First, *realize*; second, *recognize*; and finally *respond*. As a believer, you must *realize* your position, then *recognize* the perils that are around you. And finally, armed with this knowledge, you must do something about it, or *respond* to that prospect or the opportunity.

REALIZE OUR POSITION

As we consider our spiritual battle, let's go back to 1 Chronicles 12:32. The men are called "sons of Issachar." While we may understand these words, together they might not mean much to us, but they could be simply translated, "These were just ordinary guys in this tribe." Yet these ordinary people made themselves available at an extraordinary time for extraordinary purposes. Throughout the Scriptures God makes extraordinary use of ordinary people. Notice these sons of Issachar are only two hundred of a group of people that is a small number in comparison to the groups listed in the previous two verses. They are not the 20,800 from the tribe of Ephraim mentioned in verse 30, nor are they the 18,000 men from the half-tribe of Manasseh mentioned in verse 31. The leaders of Issachar were a much smaller group, yet they understood their times and knew what Israel ought to do. They were a few regular folk who possessed exceptional insight and direction.

5

I'm convinced that for our day we need more "sons and daughters of Issachar," or individuals who understand what's going on in our world and know what to do about it. Look around you because these men and women of Issachar can be anyone who dares to have the kind of insight and vision that only God can provide.

A great Chinese legend talks about a group of elderly cultured Chinese gentlemen who periodically liked to meet together. These men would drink tea and share wisdom with each other. Various men in the group took turns displaying the tea. Besides sharing wisdom, the man in charge of the tea was required to locate the most exotic blends of tea. To impress the others, they only used the rarest and most costly teas.

One day it was the turn of the most venerated and respected gentleman in that group to host the tea party. With great ceremony and pomp, he placed the tea in a little gold box and measured it out with a gold spoon. This created an amazing presentation. Each one of the elderly men drank their tea and commented on its exquisite flavor. This tea was unlike anything they had ever tasted. At that point the elderly host of the group said, "This tea which you have found so delightful is the same tea that our peasants drink. There is no difference. I hope this experience is a reminder that all good things in life are not necessarily the rarest or the most costly."

If you are a son or daughter of Issachar, you possess great wisdom, yet you are also a son or a daughter of God. It's the God-element that makes you extraordinary and gives you an edge that others don't possess. God will use anyone who makes themselves available and says, "God, use me." First Corinthians 1:26-28 says:

For you see your calling, brethren, that not many wise according to the flesh, not many mighty, not many noble, are called. But God has chosen the foolish things of the world to put to shame the wise, and God has chosen the weak things of the world to put to shame the things which are mighty; and the base things of the world ... to bring to nothing the things that are.

Here's my point: God isn't necessarily looking for the Phi Beta Kappas, the politicians, the nobility, the world-famous athletes, or the statesmen. The Lord will take anyone. He can use those famous people, But understand that God is not saying, "I hang my hat on that kind of person." Instead He is saying, "I just want anyone who, as my son or daughter, will step into this arena of insight and vision and do something about it." While we are sons and daughters of the flesh, more importantly we are sons and daughters of the living God.

First Chronicles 12:32 warns that there are dangers involved when it states that these sons of Issachar "had understanding of the times." What does that mean? These people understood exactly what they were up against and knew the dangers of the time in which they were living. Saul was a jealous, angry, and vengeful king who wanted to kill David. Because the people of Issachar aligned with David, they understood it brought danger to them. Ultimately, they knew David, not Saul, was going to be the king, but as they stepped in to help David become the king, this choice meant possible death for them. The sons of Issachar understood their times.

In the same way, we need to understand our times, discerning who is the real enemy and what he is doing. We need to know the attacks and assaults that are being mounted around us. Because the world is confused, they don't know the identity of the real enemy, what is going on, nor what they need to do about it. You and I do have this understanding—or at least we should.

To the religious leaders of his day, in Matthew 16, Jesus said, "How is it that you can discern the face of the sky, but you can't discern the signs of the times?" (see verse 3). Then He repeated His point, saying, "You're great at weather maps. You can forecast the weather but you can't foresee the future or even focus on the present. You don't know what's happening around you." And yet they should have been able to understand the sign of the times.

That was during the time of Jesus, but what about us today? What are the big issues that we face? The chapters that follow will provide important details about these issues.

THE TOP OF THE LIST: ETERNAL INSECURITY

Let's begin with the most important issue, the one that tops the list. I call it eternal insecurity. The majority of people who surround us don't really care about eternity. Instead, their focus is on their kids, or college for their kids, or their future plans, or their physical security. I doubt anyone except for perhaps a few people is even seriously thinking about eternity.

In fact, when you ask people about eternity, this topic seems to be filled with a big question mark. Some people label themselves as agnostics and say, "I just don't know what happens after we die." These people have eternal insecurity. Surveys show half of American adults say that if a person is generally good or does good things then they'll earn a place in Heaven. This statistic holds even if you ask a follow-up question about how they would define *Heaven*, as they are a little at a loss to define it. Yet 51 percent of Americans say they're searching for meaning and purpose in life. About the same number of people, or another third of Americans, don't belong to a church. They believe Satan is not real, that he only symbolizes evil instead of being a real entity.[1] The world without Christ feels eternally insecure because most of them have no concept of eternal security. In fact, they *should* feel that way because outside of Jesus Christ, there is no eternal security.

Here's the danger: Some people don't feel eternal security because they believe something like, "I'll be a good person and make it into Heaven." When it comes to feeling eternally insecure, you may be surprised to learn some individuals inside the Church also feel insecure. Why? These people are insecure about their own faith, their own relationship with God, and their own salvation. They say things like, "I know I was saved, but I don't know if I still am saved. I think I've lost my salvation, and I can't find it." These people feel they have to be born again over and over, because they haven't performed all of the works that make them a good person.

Recently, a leader was talking about an interesting study from Kentucky. He said, "Sixty-four percent of Kentucky's Southern Baptists believe they need to continually work toward salvation or risk losing it." Then this leader lamented, "We have just not done a great job in teaching one of the key doctrines of our faith."

Whether we are in the Church or outside of the Church, there is an eternal insecurity about our stance with God. It's tragic because John the Apostle said that Christians should be certain. First John 5:13 says: "These things I have written to you who believe in the name of the Son of God, that you may know that you have eternal life." Every believer needs to know that they are secure in Christ.

THE NEXT ISSUE: FAMILY IRRESPONSIBILITY

The second greatest area of homeland security deals with the family. If it weren't bad enough that we have eternal insecurity, we also have family irresponsibility. You don't have to look far to understand that for some time the family has been under attack. As I consider the family in our society today, I fear some of us are caving in to political and societal pressure. As a country, the government is worried about border security, including who is crawling over the border fence or under it. Don't get me wrong, because border security is a viable concern. But when we look at the issue of real homeland security, I believe we're not worried enough about our homes, our families, and our marriages. The family ought to matter more to us than the border of the nation.

Social scientist James Wilson said, "We are witnessing a profound worldwide long-term change in the family that's likely to continue for a long time." He said, "The scale of marital breakdown in the West since the 1960s has no historical precedent."[2] Do you understand what that means? He is saying, "I can't find any other period of time in history that parallels the kind of time we're seeing in the West in terms of the breakdown of the marriage and the family. None."

Some of you may be thinking, *Oh, here he goes again.* But see if you agree with this statement: *When I was a kid, everyone knew the definition of a family. You didn't have to define it as a husband and a wife with or without children.* Today it's not so easy to define the family. Politicians can't even agree on the definition of a family. In fact, they're so skittish about giving a definition that they want to include everyone, which is impossible.

I want you to read the words of a sociologist and historian named Karl Zimmerman from 1947. While his words were written over fifty years ago, Zimmerman seems almost prophetic because he wrote about what he saw in cultures and civilizations. He concluded that when civilizations declined, there was always an interesting parallel of a declining family structure. He said, "There are things endemic in any civilization that is going down the tubes." There are certain patterns that are the same. Let me share some of these ideas. "Marriage loses its sacredness, it's frequently broken by divorce, the traditional meaning of the marriage ceremony is lost, feminine movements abound, there's an increased disrespect for parents and authority in general, there's a growing desire for an acceptance of adultery, there's an increase in and spread of sexual perversions and sex-related crimes, and a refusal of people with traditional marriages to accept family responsibilities." If this quotation from 1947 isn't a wake-up call for us today, then I don't know what it would be. Our families are in crisis.

FIGHTING CULTURAL CONFORMITY

The third issue that concerns our homeland security is cultural conformity. As believers in the Kingdom of Christ, we are called to live different lives. And in Romans 12:2, Paul wrote: "Do not be conformed to this world, but be transformed by the renewing of your mind." The Moffatt translation of Romans 12:2 says: "Don't do what the world does. Don't let the world squeeze you into its own mold." If you are living differently, then you are not conformed to the culture. How are you doing in that department? Consider your church and your Christian friends. Are you living differently from your culture?

We spend thousands of dollars on home security systems. There is nothing wrong with this expense, for it is wise to protect our property. There are elaborate security systems with triggers on windows and doors. When the alarm goes off, it sounds throughout the neighborhood and the police come. Here's the irony to me: While we worry about protecting our *possessions*, we don't expend the energy to protect the *people* who live in our homes. Most of us have little holes in the walls of our houses. I call them "soul thieves" because they steal souls. Through those little holes runs a cable that carries television signals and the Internet into your house. Cable TV and the Internet display many different values, ideas, humor, and images that are being pumped into your home and in front of your children, stealing their souls and, in some respects, your own.

Christians spend seven times as much time on entertainment as they do on spiritual activities. This uneven proportion shows up in our changed values. The George Barna Group says one-third of born-again Christian adults say abortion is morally acceptable. A large number of these born-again believers feel that living with someone outside of the bonds of marriage is perfectly acceptable. As these soul thieves enter your home, some of them are attached to the porn industry and create a huge problem, which is only growing worse. Porn is a $13.3 billion per year industry. Just let that number sink in: $13.3 billion. For the men, I want to frame this for you in a context. The porn industry has a greater revenue than the revenues of the NBA, the NFL, and Major League Baseball *combined*. Some of you reading these pages are involved in pornography, and you need to stop it because it's eroding your families, as well as your own heart.

SPIRITUAL ANIMOSITY

As we look at our homeland security, another area of concern is what I call spiritual animosity. Even for those of us inside the walls of the Church, an aggressive, vocal group of people are even more aggressive and vocal against us. Persecution of Christians in the world is worse than ever before; in fact, worldwide, it is worse in the twentieth century than in all combined previous centuries. I'm speaking about the United States of America. Books like *The God Delusion* and *God Isn't Great*, or the film *The Golden Compass*, are all engineered to dismantle people's faith in God, especially in the Lord Jesus Christ.

Immediately following September 11, 2001, I noticed this trend in its beginning stages. People said things like, "These fundamentalist groups have attacked our country and the Towers fell. Who are these people that caused such destruction?" And then the rhetoric started about fundamentalism: both fundamentalist Islams and fundamentalist Christian—"radicals" who really believe in their holy books. I thought, *Very soon they're going to lump us all together, saying, "Fundamentalist anything is all evil, all bad."* And the statistics validate my impression. Over half, or 56 percent of the atheists and agnostics in America believe *radical Christianity* is as threatening to America as *radical Islam*.[3] This means if you dare believe the Bible is real and you live by the truth of the Scriptures, then you are suspect. It's what I mean by *spiritual animosity*. The typical profile of the atheist is young, educated, and vocal.

I ask, "Why aren't we vocal about our faith?" In fact, we are afraid to be vocal and so we say things like, "We don't want to say Jesus is the only way because it could offend someone." There are many other loud voices in our culture, whether it be radical Islam or the homosexual community or the atheists. Christians should be able to say in simple terms, "This is what I believe, and I won't change. But God can change you, and He loves you. God has a plan for you and your life." Don't back down.

INTERNATIONAL INSTABILITY

There are many areas of homeland security that we will cover in this book, but in this opening chapter, I want to cover one final issue: international instability. As believers in Jesus Christ, we are unique: There really are people out there who want to destroy us. Jesus told us that we would hear of wars and rumors of war. What are we to make of these rumors, and during such a time, where can we find peace, stability, and security? Consider for a moment the religion of Islam. Does Islam have an agenda, or is it fabricated? As Christians, what do we know about it and how can we respond with reason and righteousness?

Recently the government of Great Britain decided to banish the phrase *war on terror*. They decided they couldn't use those words any longer because they were too discriminating. Despite the fact that that nation has experienced several terrorist attacks, they still don't want to pinpoint a certain group, persuasion, or religion as being at fault. Instead, they call terrorist acts "random murders" and say that many are unrelated. I know for certain that toning down our rhetoric won't make this problem go away. We need to understand these trends in our culture and the common thread among them. Each of them is real, and we need to understand that. However, at the same time, each of these trends is slow-growing. As we take our kids to school, get a job promotion, and move to a different town, these steady trends continue to erode our culture. If you've ever lived on a coast, you understand the concept of erosion. While the best view of the ocean is an ocean view, everyone who lives on the edge knows that today's ocean view may be tomorrow's ocean. Their homes could go down and disappear as the coastline erodes. In the same way, these various issues have an eroding effect on our culture.

I want to conclude this chapter with a focus on hope. Each of us needs to understand our position in Christ. As ordinary people who are sons and daughters of God, the Lord of the universe has enlisted us for an extraordinary task. Next, we need to recognize the dangers, the things that are going on in our world. We want to be informed. Finally, we need to be prepared with a response from the Scriptures. We don't want to say, "Yeah, I'm doing a whole bunch of reading and I agree that it's bad out there." The important thing is, how should you respond? We see the answer in the last part of 1 Chronicles 12:32.

Let's put it all together. A group of two hundred men had vision, perspective, insight, and perception. Based on their vision, they held an important strategy to be people whom God could use in mighty ways. As you follow me and work through these issues of homeland security, I'll be giving you strategic tools you will need for success.

We need to be informed, equipped, and engaged. If you are informed, then you are reading. Remember that word? *Read.* In this country, a long time ago, reading had a high value. Yet the visual image has usurped our value for the printed page. It's true that people don't read as much anymore. I'm asking you to read more and find out what's going on. You especially need to read your Bible and discover the big picture from God about what's going on. Then you will be equipped to face your world and your culture. You *can* protect yourself, and you will also know how to promote Christ to those around you.

I'm not asking us to just circle the wagons in the sphere of believers. We can't just stop with a desire to protect ourselves and our families. That is a beginning, but we want to move beyond this fortress mentality. We want to look for creative ways to insert the gospel message into our everyday lives.

Then we will be engaged in our world and know we are all in this together. I often quote what Edmund Burke once said: "All that is necessary for evil to triumph is for good people to do nothing."

Back in the 1950s, Tommy Bolt was a professional golfer with a name that resonated in the golf community. While in Los Angeles for a match, everyone in golf knew that Tommy Bolt's caddy was a chatterbox who just talked throughout the whole game. Before Tommy teed off, he turned to his caddy and said, "Okay, in this game you don't say a word unless I ask you. Then you say either yes or no. Got it?"

"Yes." So Tommy swung, took his tee shot, and then he walked out to the fairway to find the ball. He located the ball under a tree and a bit off the fairway. To make the tough shot, he had to shoot underneath the tree, over a lake, and onto the green. He looked at the shot and then turned to his caddy and asked, "Five iron, don't you think?"

The caddy stood there and said, "No."

Tommy Bolt said, "What do you mean, not a five iron? Watch this." He grabbed a five iron and made the perfect shot, which went under the tree, over the lake, and onto the green, landing about two feet from the cup. As he handed the club to his caddy, he said, "What do you think of that? You can talk now."

The caddy replied, "Mr. Bolt, you just hit the wrong ball."

Oh, can you imagine? He made a perfect shot with the other guy's golf ball.

Today is the time for God's people to get into the right game. Many of us are just swinging at stuff. Learn what you are to aim at, get into the game, and evaluate your life. Some of you are very good at what you do professionally and in the community. I'm glad for that excellence. In the pages of this book, I'm asking you to evaluate your actions in light of this question: *Am I making an eternal impact?*

Chapter 2

SECURE THE FOUNDATIONS

One of the most famous landmarks in the world is the Leaning Tower of Pisa. If you haven't been to visit it in person, you've probably seen a picture or at least heard about the structure. The Leaning Tower is remarkable, but not because of its height. At 179 feet tall, there are many taller structures, and while the tower is a marvelous example of Romanesque architecture, that's not why it is famous. While it is 835 years old, the reason for its fame is that it leans; not only does it lean, but it is eventually going to fall. Since 1911, they've measured its descent and known the structure drops 1/20 of an inch every single year. It is now to the point that it's seventeen feet out of plumb. In 2007, experts predicted it would collapse, yet it still stands, and in this chapter, I will tell you why it is still there. The word *Pisa* means "marshy ground"—and the city was formed on this type of soil. This gives you a clue why the tower started to lean—even before the building was completed! The Leaning Tower of Pisa has a weak foundation, only nine feet deep, yet it is 179 feet high. My dad was a builder, and he would say that a building is only as good as its foundation. It's the same with life—our lives are only as good as their foundations.

As we consider our foundations, let's read the words of Jesus in the Sermon on the Mount:

> "Not everyone who says to Me, 'Lord, Lord,' shall enter the kingdom of heaven, but he who does the will of My Father in heaven. Many will say to Me in that day, 'Lord, Lord, have we not prophesied in Your name, cast out demons in your name, and done many wonders in Your name?' And then I will declare to them, 'I never knew you; depart from Me, you who practice lawlessness!' Therefore whoever hears these sayings of Mine, and does them, I will liken him to a wise man who built his house on the rock: and the rain descended, the floods came, and the winds blew and beat on that house; and it did not fall, for it was founded on the rock. But everyone who hears these sayings of Mine, and does not do them, will be like a foolish man who built his house on the sand: and the rain descended, the floods came, and the winds blew and beat on that house; and it fell. And great was its fall." (Matthew 7:21-27)

In the pages of this chapter, you will learn about the most important thing in our lives: spiritual security. When your soul is under attack and you are looking for homeland security, remember that your personal eternal security is the most vital issue in the long run. What good is it to protect your borders, your homeland, your family, and your home if your soul is in peril? As Jesus said: "What will it profit a man if he gains the whole world, and loses his own soul?" (Mark 8:36). Matthew 5, 6, and 7 comprise the most famous message from Jesus Christ, known as the Sermon on the Mount. If you have a Bible that has printed the words of Jesus in red, you will find these entire chapters are red because the words are only from Jesus Christ. The words I just quoted are found at the end of His message; it is His application point. For His listeners, Jesus was summing up with His points, admonishing His listeners to obey. And here's why: The crowd listening to Jesus on that day wasn't a pagan or heathen crowd. By and large these people acknowledged God; many of them were Jewish, and most of them probably attended synagogues around Galilee. You might say they had a form of godliness. Any life needs to be built on a strong foundation, but their lives were leaning. Aware of their spiritual condition, Jesus warned them in this Sermon on the Mount.

When I was around ten years old, I got really concerned about dying and eternity. Because a friend of the family died, I was worried about what would happen when I died. For some answers, I sought a priest of the church I attended and asked, "What's going to happen when I die? Am I going to go to Heaven?"

I'll never forget his response: "Well, nobody really knows until they die."

As a ten-year-old kid, I was thinking, *At that point, it's too late to find out you're wrong! Isn't there a way to know for sure?*

From my years of studying the Scriptures, I can assure you that we *can* know for certain where we will go when we die. We are going to deal with eternal security as a doctrine in the next chapter. In this chapter, we are still considering how to build your life on the right foundation. Some people have a *false* sense of security because they trust in themselves. Others have a *flimsy* sense of security because they disobey

21

Christ. But others have a *firm* sense of security, or a solid foundation, and that's where we want to end up. We're going to take some time and examine each of these three distinct groups, some of whose lives, Jesus said, didn't reflect their words; they were missing the important things in life.

In Matthew 7:21, let's examine this false security that some will have: "Not everyone who says [notice that, it's professing something with their lips] to Me, 'Lord, Lord,' shall enter the Kingdom of Heaven, but he who does the will of My Father in heaven" (words in brackets added). Immediately we're dealing with a group of people who acknowledge the good Lord. They're saying, "Lord," and even using it twice; in the next verse, as well, they say, "Lord, Lord." The double use of this word emphasizes their passion or fervor. Besides using the word *Lord*, there is a threefold repetition of the words "in your name." As Christians, we have our own vocabulary. Early on when I was a Christian, I noticed this language. It's not necessarily a bad thing for the brand-new Christian, though it is a little disarming. I recall the first time I heard someone say, "Praise the Lord!" followed by "Thank you, Jesus!" followed by "Glory to God, hallelujah!"

Because I wasn't used to such expressions, I honestly thought it was weird. And for some Christians it's like turning on the faucet and letting the water run. These expressions just kept going and going and going. Later my perspective on these expressions has changed, and what I originally thought was weird, I came to see as beautiful. "Praise the Lord" is a beautiful acknowledgment of Jesus as the Lord. When someone uses the phrase "Lord, Lord," it means they are willing to submit to the Lord. But while the verbal profession is good, the person's life needs visual proof or it's not good. As James 2:17 said so succinctly: "Faith by itself, if it does not have works, is dead."

Over a third of all Americans, 35 percent, use the term *born again* when referring to themselves, yet only 7 percent of that group are evangelicals. Some people use the term *born again* just because they have heard it before, not because they really know what it means. Some people can speak "Christianese," but they don't have eternal life. Billy Graham said, "Our evangelistic crusades find both the greatest challenge and the greatest response among church members." Here's my point: It's not good enough to talk about God. If that's all you have, it's a false security. Observe something else in this verse: Besides their acknowledgment of the good Lord, they affirmed other good words. Jesus said, "Many will say to Me in that day, 'Lord, Lord, have we not prophesied in Your name?'"

Next, Jesus issued a warning to the pulpit, directly toward those who speak *for* God, not just *about* God. These people prophesy in the name of Jesus or represent God at some level as spokesmen and women for the Lord.

You may ask, "Is it possible for a spokesperson for the Lord, such as a pastor or a ministry leader, to still need this warning today?" It is absolutely possible. Acts 18 in the New Testament tells about a man named Apollos, who was an Alexandrian Jew and was described as "an eloquent man and mighty in the Scriptures" (Acts 18:24). This chapter tells us that Apollos could preach, yet his speaking was incomplete. Because he was taught the baptism of John the Baptist, or water baptism, Apollos believed Jesus was only a good man, a moral and ethical teacher. Someone took Apollos aside and explained the fullness of the message to him. Until then, Apollos was a spokesperson for God, yet he was not saved until he gained the full understanding about Jesus Christ.

Several years ago Christmas Day fell on a Sunday that I will never forget. During the Sunday morning church service, I gave an invitation for people to receive Christ. From the left side of the congregation, an older gentleman walked forward with tears in his eyes. At the end of the service I asked, "Can you tell me your story?"

He said, "For years I've been an elder in a church, yet I have not known Jesus Christ until just a few moments ago when I prayed to invite Him into my life." This spokesperson for God, an elder of a church, didn't actually know Christ. Ironically one great hero of the Church, Martin Luther, had the same testimony. Concerned about his soul, Martin Luther joined a monastery in Erfurt, Germany, where he was eventually ordained to the priesthood, studied theology, became a doctor of theology, taught the Scriptures, and taught theology. Yet from his own testimony, Martin Luther said at that time he was not a believer. My key point is that *talking about* God is good and *talking for* God is good, yet if there is nothing more, then there is only false security. In the Sermon on the Mount, Jesus said some people acknowledged the good Lord, not only with good words but also through good works: "[They say,] 'Lord, Lord, have we not prophesied in Your name, [get this] cast out demons in Your name, and done many wonders [*dunamis*, powerful acts] in Your name?" (Words in brackets added.)

Is it possible for someone who is either a nominal believer or unregenerate to do this? How do you explain this verse? Here are three possibilities. First, the works were done in the name of Jesus yet with the power of Satan. I know this concept can mess with your thinking a bit, so let's dig into it some more. Acts 8 describes Simon, a sorcerer, who lived in a region called Samaria. Because Simon did powerful, miraculous works, everyone said, "This man is using the great power of God," yet the Bible says the powerful acts were done by the power of the devil. Also, Acts 19 tells us of the seven sons of Skeva in Ephesus who were Jewish exorcists. These brothers had heard of Jesus Christ and had seen the power of using Jesus' name, so they tried to use this power for themselves. They would say, "In the name of Jesus Christ whom Paul preaches," when they cast out demons. Finally, the Bible says that in the end times there will be the Antichrist, who will come with "the working of Satan, with all power, signs, and lying wonders" (2 Thessalonians 2:9). These different examples reveal the possibility of someone who is a nominal believer or not even a believer doing great things for God.

There is a second explanation for this verse. While the people were nominal believers or even unbelievers, it was an exception and not a rule that the power of God worked through them. This explanation disturbs our thinking because we want everything to be cut and dried. Remember in Numbers 22, a man named Balaam was a false prophet, not a Hebrew prophet; he didn't know God. Balaam believed in a pagan religion, yet when he spoke, God put His words in Balaam's mouth so that he could only bless Israel. The restraining power of God made Balaam act in this manner. Or consider Caiaphas, the high priest who did not believe in Jesus, yet who at the Crucifixion of Christ said, "It is expedient for us that one man should die for the people" (John 11:50). The gospel writer adds a footnote that says that Caiaphas was prophesying that Jesus Christ would die as atonement. These examples are illustrations of this second possibility.

Finally, there is a third option. The group of people whom Jesus mentioned only professed their belief, but it was not authentic. You can talk about God, talk for God, and be doing good things for God, yet it provides a false sense of security if there is nothing more to it. The false security will turn into a flimsy security when a person with that attitude tries to face the judgment of God. It is like someone who makes the right speech but is missing the right attitude of the heart. The Leaning Tower will eventually collapse. The missing element is pointed out in Matthew 7:23, in which Jesus said: "And then I will declare to them, 'I never knew you.'" For just a moment, let those words sink in.

Jesus continued, "Depart from Me, you who practice lawlessness" (Matthew 7:23). This group is missing two elements. They are saying the right words, yet they are missing the lifestyle and the practice. When Jesus said they were practicing lawlessness, in the Greek language He used the present participle, which simply means a continual action. A better translation would be, "Depart from me, you who continually or habitually are practicing lawlessness." Here's the point: Anyone who continually practices sin gives evidence that they don't belong to Christ.

Now you may be saying, "Now wait a minute, Skip. Don't Christians sin?" Yes, they do. "Don't Christians fall?" Yes, we do, don't we? And thankfully we have forgiveness. You might even add, "Don't Christians sometimes deliberately sin?" Yes, they do, and sometimes a stronghold has a grip on a Christian's life. But if the person is a true believer, then he or she will hate the sin and wrestle with it. Yes, they will struggle with it and fight against it in a war between the flesh and the spirit. Here's the critical difference: A Christian is someone to whom sin clings while an unbeliever is someone who clings to sin. Or as someone said, "If your religion hasn't changed you, maybe it's time to change your religion."

Luke 6 provides a parallel passage to the Sermon on the Mount we've been studying in Matthew 7. Jesus said: "Why do you call Me 'Lord, Lord,' and not do the things which I say?'" (Luke 6:46). Notice how Luke emphasized the absence of a spiritual lifestyle. They had the right speech, but they missed the right actions or lifestyle.

I read a newspaper article about a doctor who was arrested for malpractice. This man wasn't a real doctor, although he hung up a shingle calling himself an MD. He had only finished three years, not four years, of medical school. He was caught because he misdiagnosed, then mistreated, a patient. To all appearances, this man looked like a doctor, but in his practice, he acted like a third-year medical student.

Erma Bombeck once wrote, "Never go to a doctor whose houseplants have died." Isn't that good advice? Are you going to turn to a "Christian" for direction if that person seems lost themselves? You can speak the right words, but you're missing the right actions, and on a fundamental level, you don't have a personal relationship with Jesus. Once again, closely examine Matthew 7:23, in which Jesus said: "I will declare to them, 'I never knew you.'"

Jesus was not saying, "I never knew *of* you." Nor was He saying, "I never got your name. What's your name again?" Instead Jesus was saying, "I never knew you as my disciples. You never knew me as your Lord, and we've never had an acquaintance." One of the most important keys to understand is that your lifestyle does not produce a relationship. It's the exact opposite—your relationship produces your lifestyle.

You can't say, "I'm going to keep doing 'spiritual' things because if I do then I will have a relationship with God." No. Your relationship with God comes first. As you meet Him, receive Him, and get to know Him then your lifestyle will flow from that relationship. The relationship comes first, and then the Christian lifestyle follows.

To have a relationship with Jesus, you've got to be in the family. How do you get in the family? To join a family, you have to be born or adopted into it. That's why Jesus said, "You must be born again to enter the kingdom of heaven." (See John 3:3.) If you're not born again, you won't enter the Kingdom of Heaven. The Apostle Paul used that beautiful picture of adoption to show that we are adopted into the family as God's children. In a sense God says, "If you receive Christ, you're born into my family."

James 2:20 explains that faith without works is dead. The reverse is also true—works without faith is also dead. You need faith, and that faith, or a relationship with Christ, will produce works. Saving faith is a faith that works and produces the evidence. In John 17, Jesus said in His prayer to His Father, "You've given eternal life to as many as you have given to me. And this is eternal life, that they may know you, the only true God and Jesus Christ, whom you have sent." (See verses 2-3.)

I was eighteen years old when I was saved. I can remember when I was two weeks old in the Lord; I confess that I was ignorant. In my closet were a couple of lids of marijuana, and I didn't see anything wrong with it. I was so ignorant about my relationship with Jesus. I did legitimately give my life to Christ. Although I loved Jesus, I smoked a little before I read the Bible. I got amazing insights, yet in my ignorance, I didn't see anything wrong with it.

One day I was reading the version of the Bible, *Good News for Modern Man*, and I reached Jesus' Sermon on the Mount. I have a vivid memory of light coming into the room. In this modern translation of Matthew 5, I read: "Happy are those whose greatest desire is to do what God requires" (verse 6 TEV). I stopped there because it felt like the Holy Spirit had just reached through the words of the page and slapped me upside the head. As I meditated on this verse, I asked, "Is my greatest desire in life to do what God requires?" In all honesty, I thought, *It hasn't been.*

I had prayed and believed I was saved, but there was something missing because I was still living in disobedience. Suddenly the thought came, *I've got to flush the marijuana in the closet down the toilet.* I threw the dope in the toilet and flushed it. I learned that a relationship with God comes first, then the lifestyle, and finally the obedience. When you learn something, you respond to it.

As we approach the final portion of our text in Matthew 7, I want you to note the reference about a coming storm in verses 24 through 27. Two houses were built, and then the wind blew and the rains came down. One house stood and the other house fell. Often when people read these verses, their interpretation is something like, "These are the storms in life. Everyone goes through trials and hard times. If you trust in Christ, you'll be able to stand and make it through."

While this is an interesting interpretation and the statement is true that we need to trust Christ for our strength, it is not the true meaning of these verses. In these verses, Jesus is referring to a particular kind of coming storm, the storm of judgment. God's wrath is coming. You can understand the type of storm in light of the context of Matthew 7:22: "Many will say to Me in that day." What is "that day"? That day is Judgment Day, when men will face Christ to give an account of their lives. As Jesus continued in Matthew 7:23: "And I will declare to them [on the same day], 'I never knew you; depart from Me, you who practice lawlessness!" (Words in brackets added.)

Can you see why it is critical to have a secure foundation? There is a storm of judgment coming. Like the Leaning Tower of Pisa, your life will fall or it will stand, depending on your foundation. Hebrews 9:27 couldn't make it any more clear: "It is appointed unto men once to die, but after this the judgment" (KJV). Hebrews 10:31 says: "It is a fearful thing to fall into the hands of the living God" (KJV).

Do you recognize the name W. C. Fields? There are a number of stories told about this actor. As W. C. Fields was in a hospital on his deathbed, one of his friends came to visit him. W. C. Fields was not a Christian and never read the Bible, yet this friend found him on his deathbed reading the Bible. His eyes were intently focused on the pages of that book. This friend was shocked and asked him, "What are you doing reading the Bible?"

Fields looked up and said, "Looking for loopholes ..."

He was going to be sorely disappointed because there aren't any loopholes except one and that is a personal relationship with Jesus Christ. Trusting Jesus is the only way to discover the exit from the coming storm of judgment.

The coming wrath of God is a major biblical theme, but it is absent from a lot of modern preaching. Today's ministers love to provide their congregations with a lot of feel-good messages that say, "Smile, God loves you. You're okay. I'm okay." From my perspective, the coming storm of God's wrath is the flip side of the gospel. The literal interpretation of the word *gospel* is "good news." Why is there good news? It's because there's been a lot of bad news about the coming storm and God's judgment.

The bright side of the gospel is captured in one of the most familiar verses in the Bible, John 3:16, which says: "For God so loved the world, that he gave his only begotten Son, that whosoever believeth in him should not perish, but have everlasting life" (KJV).

For the life of me, I don't understand why people stop at John 3:16, because they should read the whole chapter of

John 3. When you move down twenty verses to John 3:36, you discover that Jesus said: "He who believes in the Son has everlasting life; and he who does not believe the Son shall not see life, but the wrath of God abides on him."

Some people believe that the message of God's wrath is only found in the Old Testament. They say, "The God of the Old Testament is the God of wrath. If you want love, grace, or mercy, then you need to look in the New Testament." People who believe that message aren't reading their Bibles. The wrath and grace of God are themes throughout the entire Bible. Romans 1:18 says: "The wrath of God is being revealed from Heaven against all the godlessness and wickedness of men who suppress the truth by their wickedness" (NIV).

Through a continual revelation, God's wrath is being revealed from Heaven. It's another reason to celebrate the good news of the gospel. There is a way of escape from God's judgment, yet you must have the right foundation.

I find a single word in Matthew 7:22 to be haunting. The word is *many*, and it should stop everyone dead in their tracks. Jesus said, "Many will say to Me in that day, 'Lord, Lord.'" That isn't a *few* people, but *many*. Look back a few verses to Matthew 7:13-14, where Jesus explained, "Enter by the narrow gate; for wide is the gate and broad is the way that leads to destruction, and there are many who go in by it. Because narrow is the gate and difficult is the way which leads to life, and there are few who find it." These verses are sobering and shocking.

You could be making the right speech but missing the right elements. Are you building a lifestyle that is based on a relationship with Jesus? We need to be mindful of our steps throughout life. As we finish this chapter, let's look at the last few verses of Matthew 7, where Jesus said:

"Therefore whoever hears these sayings of Mine, and does them, I will liken him to a wise man who built his house on the rock: and the rain descended, the floods came, and the winds blew and beat on that house; and it did not fall, because it was founded on the rock. But everyone who hears these sayings of Mine and does not do them, will be like a foolish man who built his house on the sand; and the rain descended, the floods came, and the winds blew and beat on that house: and it fell."

The last sentence emphasizes the disastrous consequences: "Great was its fall." Wow.

Jesus has told us about two houses that have some similarities. First, each builder wanted a secure house. Second, they probably built in the same area because as the storm blew through, it affected both of the houses. Third, I expect these two houses probably looked alike on the outside. They each had a door, windows, and perhaps even a two-camel garage. From the outside, these houses were similar. The distinction was in their foundation, which you could not see.

Here's the application of this passage: When you look at someone on the outside, you can't tell the difference between a secure life and an insecure life, or between a saved person and an unsaved person. You can't point to someone and say, "That man's saved because he's smiling." That's not enough. Nor can you say, "Well, she's a Christian because she is carrying a Bible."

I've known seminary professors who taught the Bible as literature. These professors carried a Bible, yet they didn't believe a word of it. What you see on the outside isn't what is real. The reality is, what does a person have for their foundation? A real Christian takes three steps that are evident from these verses in Mathew 7: knowing, hearing, and obeying.

Matthew 7:23 points to the necessity of *knowing* the Lord. Jesus said, "I never knew you." Have you met Christ? Here's the truth: Once you meet Him, you're going to love Him. And if you love Him, you're going to want to hear what He has to say. And when you hear what He says because you love Him, you're going to want to do what He says. You will form a relationship with Jesus because you need to know Him.

Second, you need to *hear* Jesus. This is an ongoing process. In Matthew 7:24, Jesus said, "Whoever hears these sayings of Mine." Each day, I encourage you to hear Jesus and read your Bible. If you don't have a Bible, then get one. We need to listen to Him, because if God reveals himself through the Scriptures, how are you going to ever have a relationship with Him if you don't read it? As God reveals himself, that's how we develop our relationship and hear Him. You can hear God when you come to church, but I know not everyone in the church comes to hear Jesus. A couple of weeks ago, a young man told me, "There are a lot of cute girls here." He made it clear why he had come to church, and it wasn't to hear or to see God. As you come to church, expect that God is going to speak to you and carry your Bible with you. I tell my congregation to bring their Bibles, not to make them feel guilty, but because I want them to follow the message as I speak. As you increase your use of the Bible, you may need to refer to these passages and know where they are in your Bible.

The final step for a real Christian is *obedience*. In Matthew 7:24, Jesus said, "Whoever hears ... and does." Obedience comes from building a relationship. When all three elements of knowing, hearing, and doing are present, then you have built a secure life.

As I promised in the opening pages of this chapter, I want to return to the story about the Leaning Tower of Pisa. The scientists who were measuring the slow decline of the tower predicted, "The Leaning Tower of Pisa will fall in the year 2007." The tower was aimed toward a restaurant, and they said it would land there during 2007. This restaurant is where these scientists meet each year to discuss the fall of the Leaning Tower of Pisa. Oddly enough, the tower didn't fall because they temporarily fixed it. The scientists were able to move the tower back eighteen inches to its 1823 position. They've updated their date for the fall and predict it will collapse in the year 2300. Eventually the tower will fall because the foundation is weak.

In your life today, you may have nothing catastrophic or out of the ordinary happen tomorrow or this week or this month. In fact, your life may even prosper and get better. But if your life isn't built on the solid rock, like that tower, you will eventually fall. When the storm of judgment comes, great will be your fall. Each of us needs to build on the right foundation. Know Him. Hear Him. Obey Him.

Chapter 3

HEAVEN-BOUND AND ENJOYING THE RIDE

During the last week-and-a-half, I've been in five different airports. I've observed two different kinds of passengers: the confirmed ticketed passenger and the standby passenger. It was easy to tell the difference between the two. The confirmed ticketed passengers were sitting down, reading the newspaper, talking to friends or relatives, working on a computer, or maybe even sleeping as they waited for their flights. Their places on the airplane were secure because they had tickets. You could tell the standby passengers because they would pace the floor or stand anxiously near the ticket counter. The distinction between these two types of passengers boils down to one word: *confidence*. Without confidence, their places on the flight were uncertain and that's why they paced.

What if in the next hour you knew that you would be standing before a holy God who would render a verdict for your eternity? How would you respond? Would you be pacing, hovering, and wondering? Or would you be confident? Would you be wondering if God was going to say, "Welcome home"? Or maybe you would be thinking the Lord would say, "Depart from me, you who work iniquity."

That's exactly what I want to talk to you about as we continue considering homeland security. I want to make sure you are "Heaven-bound and enjoying the ride." While a ticketed passenger and a standby passenger may indeed end up at the same destination, not everyone enjoys the process.

In the previous chapter we looked at some verses in Matthew 7 and discovered that a believer's personal eternal security can be found in Christ and Christ alone. The foundation of our eternal security is not from our own good works, but it begins with a personal relationship with Jesus Christ. We need to be born again and know Jesus. Then, once we know Jesus, we will love Him, hear Him, and obey Him. As we put this relationship first, then this relationship produces our lifestyle. Anyone with a personal relationship with Jesus Christ is very secure. But there's a flip side to this situation—the insecure, timid, and fearful individuals who are like the standby passengers. They are perhaps Heaven-bound, yet they're not enjoying the ride.

With this matter in mind, let's read 1 John 5:13, which is our anchor text for this chapter: "These things I have written to you who believe in the name of the Son of God, that you may know that you have eternal life, and that you may continue to believe in the name of the Son of God."

I want to read 1 John 5:13 in a different translation called the Wuest translation. Kenneth Wuest was a Greek scholar who took the original text and expanded it according to its Greek meanings. Here's his translation of 1 John 5:13: "These things I write to you in order that you may know with an absolute knowledge that the life you are having is eternal life."

The Apostle John lived in certainty and without ambiguity. He didn't use words like "I hope," but instead many times he used the words "I know." In fact, thirty-two times in this short epistle, John used the word *know*. John didn't want us to be standby passengers who hover, wait, and hope, but John wanted us to be passengers with confirmed tickets who know about our eternal destination.

Let's take 1 John 5:13 and slice it into two key questions: First, why should we be certain? And second, how can we be sure?

Let's consider the first question: Why should we be certain? Notice John says, "That you may know." Why are some people insecure about their eternal salvation? There are several different reasons. First, they are insecure because they are not saved. Their insecurity is not a good feeling; it is probably a bit haunting because they are unsure about their eternal destiny.

I had been saved for about two weeks and was giving my testimony when someone listening to me butted into the conversation and said, "How did you know you were saved?"

"That's easy," I replied. "I was there when it happened."

For some people it has never happened at all, and yet for others, they were there but it never fully happened. It is possible for some people to have had a conversion of sorts that actually fell short of a true conversion. Some people have a "ceremonial conversion." They become wrapped up in Christian ceremonies or rituals and they do certain things because they think it is what they are supposed to do. But the rituals replace true faith, authentic repentance, and real belief.

Other people have a "cultural conversion." This type of person agrees with certain Christian values and participates in certain Christian activities. They will say things like, "Going to church is good; I ought to do more of that. I have kids now; they ought to be in Sunday school and have a good influence in their lives." These individuals have made a cultural conversion instead of a true Christian conversion.

Another group of people have made a "mental" or "emotional conversion," because they were pressured into it during an emotional moment, or a relative or a fiancée talked them into a conversion. I'm not saying that the Christian faith is not reasonable. You could sit down and show these people how to make an intelligent and heartfelt commitment. But A. W. Tozer once said, "If someone could talk you into it, maybe someone smarter could talk you out of it." A true conversion is something deeper than this type of experience. Some people feel insecure because they have never been saved in the first place, which only breeds more insecurity.

Another reason some people feel insecure about their salvation is they don't know it's possible to be sure. Some Christians believe nobody can really know until they die. (The previous chapter included my exchange with a clergyman about this matter.)

Possibly you recognize the name Dr. Roy Zuck. This professor at Dallas Theological Seminary has produced one of the greatest Christian commentaries of the last several years. In Amsterdam, Roy was witnessing to a young man about Christ, and toward the end of their conversation this young man seemed to be very open. Roy said, "Do you want to pray to receive Christ?"

The young man had an interesting response: "Well, I don't know if I'm one of the elect or not."

Roy said, "When do you plan to find that out?"

"I won't know until I die if I'm one of the elect," the young man said.

"That's a little too late, isn't it," Roy said, "to find out you're wrong?"

The young man shot back, "If I die and find out that I'm not among the elect, I'll do my best to glorify God in hell." What an utterly despairing statement from a standby passenger. It would be comparable to seeing a doctor who said, "I've examined you and you may have cancer. Then again, you may not."

"How will I know?" the patient would ask.

The doctor responds, "If you die of it, then we'll know you had cancer." That type of response isn't going to help, and it definitely isn't going to comfort the patient. It's the same type of situation when you feel you have to wait to be sure of your salvation until you die. If you take this stance, then you deny God's sovereignty over salvation.

Some people feel if you know for certain that you are saved and going to Heaven, then you will be arrogant for some reason. They say, "How prideful and arrogant of you to know you're going to Heaven." But I know I'm going to Heaven because of what God has written in the Bible.

Other people contend that if you know you are saved for eternity, then you're opening the door to loose living. For some reason, because you feel secure in your salvation, you are going to lower your standards and get involved in things that you shouldn't. But Jesus said in John 5:24: "Most assuredly, I say to you, he who hears My word and believes in Him who sent Me has everlasting life." Notice Jesus didn't use words like "may have" or "hope he has" or "he'll find out if he has it when he dies." It is clear that anyone who believes has eternal life. Then Jesus continued, saying, "… and shall not come into judgment, but has passed from death into life."

The third reason some people feel insecure about their salvation is that they don't understand the grace of God. These Christians have been living under the thumb of legalism for such a long time that they don't understand grace. Anyone in this category is comparable to the Judaizers in Acts 15 who said, "Unless you are circumcised according to the custom of Moses, you cannot be saved" (verse 1). Some Christians only understand grace to be a little prayer they say before a meal.

One time an old Native American chief was led to Christ. His family began wondering about the changes in his life, so they asked him to explain. "How did you come to this understanding? Tell us why you are different."

To explain, the old chief took a little worm and put it on top of a pile of dried leaves on the ground. He lit a match to one of the leaves and it started burning. Just before the entire bundle consumed everything, including the worm, he reached down and snatched the worm. As he held the worm gently in his hand, he said, "Me, the worm." That elderly gentleman understood God's grace. My life has been transformed because God reached down, snatched me out of the flame, and now He holds me gently in His hand.

In the 1700s, an old Puritan preacher named Thomas Mantan said, "None walk so evenly with God as those who are assured of the love of God." Some people don't understand the keeping power of God's grace. They become timid and fearful, which begs this question: Why is it so important to know about your eternal salvation?

Let me give the short answer and then expand it. If you know God's grace, it will show. If you don't know God's grace, it will show. First you need to understand God's grace, and the assurance of your salvation will then produce a sense of stability. Security produces stability, while insecurity produces instability. Notice the last part of 1 John 5:13 says, "That you may continue to believe in the name of the Son of God." Your salvation produces stability in your life.

Have you ever been traveling to a place and then you take a wrong turn and get lost? You thought you were on the right path, then you discover that you were not going the right way. It depends on where you are in this process, but often you will panic. Years ago when our son, Nathan, was just a baby, I decided to put the family in the car and drive down to White Sands and then Las Cruces. I was driving down the road, thinking I knew where I was going, but then I took a wrong turn and arrived instead in a little town named Carrizozo.

If you have never been to Carrizozo, then I'm not surprised. This little wide spot in the road has no doctor within a hundred miles. Because of my wrong turn, we were in this place when our car broke down. Nathan was throwing up in the backseat of the car. I needed to get him to a doctor but no one was available. I started to panic. This type of panic can occur in the life of an insecure believer who says, "I thought I was on the right path, but maybe I'm lost." The secure Christian remembers the words from the Book of Hebrews about our hope. The writer describes it "as an anchor of the soul, both sure and steadfast" (Hebrews 6:19). That's stability.

Before a battle, General Stonewall Jackson once said, "My spiritual beliefs teach me to be as secure in the battle as I am in my own bed." That's what I call assurance! If you don't have this type of assurance, then you are a victim of circumstance. One day you're going to feel good, and then another day you're not going to feel good. One day you're going to feel close to God, and then the next day you're not going to feel as close to God. Your life will lack joy, and instead you'll be filled with anxiety and instability. Your eternal salvation is important to know because that assurance produces stability.

The second reason to be assured of your salvation is because it increases your effectiveness as a witness for Jesus Christ. You are more effective telling others about Jesus because you're sure about your own life and you want others to be sure as well. Also, your assurance will increase the effectiveness of your prayer life. Look at the next two verses, 1 John 5:14-15: "Now this is the confidence that we have in Him, that if we ask anything according to His will, He hears us. And if we know that He hears us, whatever we ask, we know that we have the petitions that we have asked of Him." Jesus taught us to pray, "Our Father in heaven." If you're not sure God is your Father, then you're not sure that He's going to answer any prayer. In fact, your prayers will be ineffective.

For example, imagine that you see a group of bikers wearing their leather jackets and sitting by the side of the road. Would you have the freedom to walk up to one of them, slap him on the back, sit on his Harley, and then demand the keys? You wouldn't if you want to live long. But what if that biker was your brother who loved you and you loved him? Then you wouldn't think twice about asking to borrow his bike. Your assurance of eternal salvation increases your effectiveness and produces stability.

We've answered the first question about why you need to have this assurance. Now let's examine the second question about how we can be sure of our eternal destiny. Let's zero in on the little phrase in 1 John 5:13: "These things I have written to you." The word *things* refers to everything that has been discussed in 1 John. In essence, John was saying, "I've just written this letter to you. The reason I've written is so you might know that you have eternal life." First John was written to help every Christian know with certainty that they are saved.

In fact, there is a fivefold test to know whether or not you are saved. Question number one: Are you obeying God's Word? Look at 1 John 2:3-5:

> Now by this we know that we know Him, if we keep His commandments. He who says, "I know Him," and does not keep His commandments, is a liar, and the truth is not in him. But whoever keeps His word, truly the love of God is perfected [or completed] in him. By this we know that we are in Him. (Words in brackets added.)

Those verses are straightforward. If you want to know whether or not you're a Christian, ask yourself if you are obeying the commands of Scripture. This question was exactly the one Jesus used when He sent out the twelve disciples and said, "Go therefore and make disciples of all the nations … teaching them to observe all things I have commanded you" (Matthew 28:19-20).

First John says, "If you obey the commandments, then you've got assurance." We know that obedience produces assurance. Someone once said, "A faith that has not changed your life has not saved your soul." Are you obeying His Word? And here's a related question to ask: How do you feel when you come up against a commandment in God's Word? I'm talking about any admonition not to do something, or a commandment for you to begin doing something, or a commandment for you to continue doing something, or a commandment to avoid something. The type of command isn't important, but how do you respond to that command when you read it? Do you automatically discount the commandment, saying, "Well, that's irrelevant and was written a long time ago. It must not mean the same today as it did back then." Or do you say simply, "I know someone else should be reading this and not me." That type of response is a deflection of the commandment. Or do you apply it to your own life and ask, "Lord, what do I need to do with this?"

I read about a Washington, DC, lawyer who called herself a religious churchgoer, who said about the commandments, "To be perfectly honest, some laws seem to apply to me and some I disregard. Some tenets of the Church add up; others are absurd and even insulting. I don't need the pope, the press, or some lowly cop to tell me how to live my life." This woman isn't very compliant when she connects to authority. Pause for a moment and consider your own attitude when you face a direct command from God's Word? Obedience to Scripture is the number-one test to know you are saved.

Here's the second test to determine your salvation: Do you believe God's truth about Jesus Christ? Specifically, do you understand the truth about who Jesus Christ is? For you to be saved, you have to believe in the right Jesus.

Many people will give lip service to their beliefs and say, "I believe in Jesus." But can you describe Him to me and add meaning to that word *Jesus*? First John 2:21-23 says:

> I have not written to you because you do not know the truth, but because you know it, and that no lie is of the truth. Who is a liar but he who denies that Jesus is the Christ? He is antichrist who denies the Father and the Son. Whoever denies the Son does not have the Father either; he who acknowledges the Son has the Father also.

Do you believe what the Bible says about the Lord Jesus Christ? Do you believe that Jesus is the only begotten Son of God, God the Son, the Messiah, and the only Savior of the world? The Bible tells us the truth about Jesus Christ. Do you believe in that Jesus? Or when you speak about Jesus, are you referring to a nice man, a good example, a wonderful teacher, plus all the words someone would teach in a *Bible as Literature* class? At times, it is laughable how our culture talks about Jesus; except eternity is no laughing matter. I'm constantly amazed at the many new ideas and theories that appear about Jesus Christ. Almost every Christmas and Easter, there are magazine articles and television programs about Jesus Christ. Over the last few years, I've watched and kept a little track record. Some people say Jesus was a magician who practiced illusion and hypnosis. Others describe Jesus as simply an illiterate artisan. Others call Jesus a zealot, while others name Him as a guru. Some people say Jesus was a world traveler, and some religions call Jesus an ascended master. I found one new perspective on Jesus from a cult in Canada that contended aliens created Jesus Christ as a human being. Most recently, a popular belief has been propogated over the last few years that Jesus was the husband of Mary Magdalene, through whom He produced a secret lineage that will eventually rule the world.

You might say, "Skip, anyone who believes that is on the fringe. It's not what most people think." You're right: It's worse. A survey of over three thousand Protestant ministers had these results: A considerable number of them have rejected altogether the idea of a personal God. They said God was the ground of all being, the force of life, and the principle of love. Among the youngest of these ministers, the majority of them does not believe in the virgin birth or regard Jesus Christ as divine in the traditional way of most Protestants. These results are frightening.

When Jesus was in Caesarea-Philippi, He asked two questions of His disciples. The first was: "Who do men say that I am?" (See Matthew 16:13.)

They gave a number of answers, such as John the Baptist or the prophet Elisha. Then Jesus asked the crucial question that is still asked today; He said, "Who do you say that I am?" (verse 15).

Peter nailed it by saying, "You are the Christ, the Son of the living God" (verse 16). This second test is a good one: Who do *you* say Jesus is?

Here's the third test for you: Are you expecting His return? First John 3:2-3 says: "Beloved, now we are children of God; and it has not yet been revealed what we shall be, but we know that when He is revealed, we shall be like Him, for we shall see Him as He is. And everyone who has this hope in Him purifies himself, just as He is pure." Every true Christian has the blessed hope that the Lord Jesus Christ will return, and we can't wait for Him to come back. Do you know why we hope for His return? As it says in 1 John 3:2: "We shall be like Him." I'm up for that.

The other day, someone asked me, "What will we look like when Jesus returns?"

I answered, "A lot better than we look right now." We're going to be like Him. Sometimes when I read the Bible, I picture John on one side of the table and the Apostle Paul on the other side of the table, because, in many cases, their writings were similar. The Apostle John wrote: "We know that when He is revealed, we're going to be like Him" (see 1 John 3:2). And Paul wrote in Philippians 3:20-21: "For our citizenship is in heaven, from which we also eagerly wait for the Savior, the Lord Jesus Christ, who will transform our lowly body that it may be conformed to His glorious body."

You can tell if someone is a real citizen of the Kingdom of God because they can't wait to see their king. The idea of Jesus' return is exciting and filled with anticipation. True Christians would love for it to happen. If you're not a true believer and learned Jesus Christ was coming back, you wouldn't be very excited. You'd say, "He is? Oh no!" A true citizen of Heaven wants to see the king, because our true citizenship is in Heaven. The longer we spend time on Earth and live as citizens of the Kingdom of God, the more we grow homesick for Heaven, because that's our real home.

During my first trip to India, I was there for three weeks. At night during the third week, I started dreaming of American food because I'd been without it for a few weeks. While I love Indian food with the curry and rice, it was so never-ending. That third week, I dreamed of hamburgers, and in India, there are no hamburgers. Because of the Hindu belief in reincarnation, they don't eat meat because they believe it could actually be your great-great-grandpa or another relative you are consuming. I was homesick for hamburgers. When I got off the airplane, I felt like Dorothy in *The Wizard of Oz*, saying, "There's no place like home. There's no place like home."

There are some people who believe it's unhealthy to expect the Lord Jesus Christ to come quickly. They say, "You can be so heavenly minded that you're no earthly good." When I hear such talk, I counter, "You're never really any earthly good until you're heavenly minded." Once you're heavenly minded, then you can live with a perspective that doesn't allow you to get wrapped up in the cares of this world. Instead you'll stay pure. Notice what 1 John 3:3 says: "Everyone who has this hope in Him [that Jesus Christ will be revealed; that He'll come] purifies himself, just as He is pure." (Words in parentheses added.) One of the most purifying ways to live is with the expectancy that at any moment Jesus could return.

While digging in the ruins of the city of Pompeii, archeologists surmised the volcano with the molten ash struck rapidly. People could see it coming, but it was too late to take action. People were found frozen in position. The majority of them were running away from the flow, such as upstairs or down into basements or trying to move to higher ground. Then they found an amazing discovery. One Roman sentinel stood by the city gate watching the flow come toward him with his hands attached to his weapon and standing upright. This soldier stood his ground and kept his guard.

This soldier is an example of how we should live our lives as believers in Jesus. We need to be prepared and ready for the Lord's return. Such a stance in your life is a good indication that you're His child. This is the third test for Christians.

We find the fourth test in 1 John: Are you conforming to God's standards? Look at 1 John 3:7-8. Get prepared because the text of this passage makes some people very uncomfortable: "Little children, let no one deceive you. He who practices righteousness is righteous, just as He is righteous. He who sins is of the devil, for the devil has sinned from the beginning. For this purpose the Son of God was manifested, that He might destroy the works of the devil." Do you see that little word *sins*? The sentence was written in the present tense and "sins" represents a continual idea. The idea behind it is to point out someone who continually and habitually practices sin. First John 3:9-10 says:

Whoever has been born of God does not [continually, habitually practice] sin, for His seed remains in him;

48

and he cannot sin [continually, habitually], because he has been born of God. In this the children of God and the children of the devil are manifest: Whoever does not practice righteousness is not of God, nor is he who does not love his brother. (Words in brackets added.)

When we become Christians, the pattern of sin is broken and a new pattern is developed. As a believer in Jesus, you gain new desires, or what the ancients used to call "holy affections." When I was a brand-new believer, I wanted to read my Bible every day to find out what it said. Before I became a Christian, I never wanted to read the Bible. Suddenly, I was reading it a great deal. Before I became a Christian, I never wanted to go to church, yet afterward I wanted to go whenever the doors were open. Before I became a believer, I never wanted to pray, yet afterward I wanted to pray. I had a completely different set of appetites, or holy affections.

The longer you are a Christian and practice conforming to God's standards, the more your sin decreases and your righteousness increases. Don't get me wrong. I'm not saying you will be perfect. No one is perfect until they reach glory and see Jesus face-to-face. Yet the general direction of your life should be toward an increase in righteousness and a decrease in sin. It doesn't mean there's not sin in your life, because your unredeemed flesh is still there. But you will know that you sin, and you will struggle with it.

If a person is unsaved, then they could care less about their habits. Unsaved people are unconcerned about God's authority over their lives. If you are saved, then you care and you struggle. While we are imperfect and we stilll fall, in general sin will decrease and righteousness will increase in our lives. One of the keys about this test is found in 1 John 3:4; it is the word *lawlessness*, which is mentioned twice: "Whoever commits sin also commits lawlessness, and sin is lawlessness." The Greek word is *anomia*, which means literally "without the law." This term refers to a person who is living as if there were no Law, someone who could not care less about what God thinks or any higher standard. In stark contrast, a true believer, while imperfect, who fails and falls, still has a desire to be more conformed to God's standards and live a holier life. If you want to be happy, then be holy.

C. S. Lewis wrote: "How little do people know who think that holiness is dull. When someone meets the real thing (that is, real holiness) it's irresistible." He continued, "If even ten percent of the world's population had it, would not the whole world be converted before the year's end?" Are you irresistible?

Here's the fifth and final test: Do you love God's children? This test is explained in 1 John 3:11-14:

> For this is the message that you heard from the beginning, that we should love one another, not as Cain who was of the wicked one and murdered his brother. And why did he murder him? Because his works were evil and his brother's righteous. Do not marvel, my brethren, if the world hates you. We know that we have passed from death to life.

And how do we know that? Because we love the brethren: "He who does not love his brother abides in death" (verse 14).

Do you care about other Christians? That's a good question to ask when you are wondering if you are really God's child. Ask yourself: Do you love God's children? Do you care about them? When you see a need, does your heart go out to them ? Do you say, "I want to meet that need?" Or do you say, "I really don't care about them, those people, or their needs"? This latter attitude would be the mark of an unsaved person, who only focuses on themselves. You could broaden this test and ask: In general do you enjoy fellowship with other Christians? Do you think, *I can't wait to get together with a group of believers and share the Word of God, sing together, pray together, and discuss spiritual things?* Or do you get together maybe once every eight months? Love is the hallmark of our fellowship with other Christians.

Dwight L. Moody said, "A doctor can be a great doctor without loving his patients. A lawyer can be a great lawyer without loving his clients. A geologist could be a good geologist without loving science. But nobody can be a good Christian without love." Do you love God's children?

There is one ultimate question from this chapter: Are you a confirmed, ticketed passenger? Or are you pacing back and forth on standby?

In 2 Corinthians 13:5, Paul said, "Examine yourselves as to whether you are in the faith. Test yourselves." If you doubt and struggle with assurance, then go back over this fivefold test and ask yourself these things: Do you love God's people? Are you looking for the return of Christ? Do you believe the things that are true and right about Jesus Christ? Is there a pattern in your life that shows you want to please and obey the Lord? If so, then breathe a sigh of relief. Allow that feeling to soothe you and calm your heart.

To conclude this chapter, let's look at 1 John 3:19 and the verses following, "By this we know that we are of the truth." That is all of the things that I just mentioned, especially loving God's children.

"By this we know that we are of the truth, and shall assure our hearts before Him. For if our heart [conscience] condemns us, God is greater than our heart, and knows all things. Beloved, if our heart does not condemn us, then we have confidence toward God" (1 John 3:19-21, words in brackets added).

The beloved Apostle John was writing so that you can have confidence toward God about your eternal destination. Some people, because of their consciences, or their hearts, are feeling weak and robbed of their joy. These believers have a tender, fearful conscience. Maybe you know someone like that. If your conscience condemns you, know that God is greater than your heart and He knows all things.

Remember when Peter denied Jesus Christ? At the time, do you think he felt pretty low? He probably said to himself, *I've committed the unpardonable sin; I've denied Jesus Christ.* After Jesus had risen from the dead in Galilee, Jesus came to Peter and three times said, "Peter, do you love me?"

Peter said, "Yes, Lord, I love you."

He asked him, "Peter! Do you love me?"

"Yes, I love you," Peter said meekly.

Jesus asked him the third time, "Peter, do you love me?"

Peter said, "Lord, you know all things and you know that I love you." We need to hold on to this thought as well about our eternal security in Jesus. God's ways are greater than our consciences. He knows all things, and He was there when your sin happened. The Lord was also present when you were converted, and He was there when you made all of those right steps. Even though you have fallen and even though your conscience is hurting and fearful, God knows all things. But the Lord of the universe wants you to know for certain. You should be sure about your salvation and you can be sure. To be very honest, if you're not saved today, I pray you'll be miserable. I pray that your conscience would be so bothersome to you that you don't get any sleep until you surrender to Christ.

You may say, "That's a horrible thing to say." No, that's a loving prayer, because I want to see you in Heaven. Also, I'm praying that those of you who know Christ will be soothed, calmed, comforted, and assured as you abide in Him. You have nothing to fear.

Chapter 4

FRACTURED FAMILIES— BROKEN LIVES

Here's a riddle for you: A perfect man met a perfect woman, and after a perfect courtship, they had a perfect wedding. And their life was, of course—perfect. One snowy and stormy Christmas Eve, this perfect couple was driving along a winding road when they noticed someone at the roadside in distress. Since they were the perfect couple, they stopped to help. There stood Santa Claus with a huge bundle of toys. Not wanting to disappoint any children on the eve of Christmas, the perfect couple loaded Santa and his toys into their vehicle. Soon they were driving along delivering the toys. Unfortunately, the driving conditions deteriorated. The perfect couple and Santa Claus had an accident, and only one of them survived.

Who was the survivor? The answer: the perfect woman. She was the only one who really existed in the first place. Everyone knows there's no Santa Claus. And there's no such thing as a perfect man. If you are a woman, you might be clapping at this point in the riddle. But I haven't finished my story. The men respond, "If there's no perfect man and there is no Santa Claus, the perfect woman must have been driving. Now we understand why there was a car accident."

There's no such thing as a perfect man. There's no such thing as a perfect woman. There's no such thing as a perfect family. Every single family has some level of malfunction. In this chapter, we're going to step into the home of a premier family in the Old Testament: that of King David, the man after God's own heart. Even King David had a strained relationship with his son Absalom. While David was a driven man with great power as king, he was a passive parent. When power and passivity combine in one individual, it creates a dangerous individual, as we'll see in this fractured family.

The family is the basic core unit of any society. History has proven that families are a barometer of society. As the family goes, so goes the society. If you have vibrant, healthy, thriving families, you have vibrant, healthy, thriving communities. Economic status doesn't matter because if you have fractured families, you will have a fractured society and culture. Powerful cultural forces are working against our families today. In fact, these forces are engaged in a fierce battle against the biblical model of a family.

You may be surprised at another force at work that is attacking the family: parents. Parents can be one of the forces that actually fight against the integrity of a family. The culture, media, fashion industry, and music lyrics, all barrage parents themselves with their messages. When young couples get married, they may not even know if they want to have children. When these couples do have children, Rick Weiss, a researcher, noted that their happiness goes down and their frustration level increases. Why? Because they have listened to messages like, "Boy, when you have a baby, it's going to change the shape of your body." Or, "You have a baby, that's going to demand a lot of time. Now your interests will have to take a backseat." It's no wonder the couple's frustration level increases and their happiness drops. Our culture sees children as an inconvenience.

One of the greatest challenges in our culture, which will only increase in the future, is the issue of abandoned children. Abandoned children are the reason for huge issues related to anger. Just consider these numbers. There are seventy million abandoned children living on the streets of our world. Two million of these children worldwide are involved in the sex trade, primarily in Asia and South America. In the United States, 1.5 million children, teenagers, and young adults are on the streets. Experts estimate that if all of the homeless youth were put together into one city, it would be the seventh largest city in America.[1] What a reality check on our world and culture! How can we secure the future generation and provide security for them? I can give one answer in two words: *parental involvement.*

Second Samuel 13 tells the story of the ruptured home of King David. As we step into their lives, we discover the relational chaos in this family. David was the father, but there was no real "Mrs. David" because there were eight wives. The king of Israel had eight wives and many concubines, or other women. From these eight wives and multiple concubines, David produced nineteen children. These nineteen children came from different mothers. Two of the children were born to him from an affair with another woman while he was married to his wives. Obviously this was a recipe for chaos.

You might be tempted to say, "In the history of that day, it was commonplace for kings to have many wives." So what? In the first book of the Bible, God declared, "For this reason a man will leave his father and mother and be united to his wife [singular], and they will become one flesh" (Genesis 2:24 NIV; word in brackets added). Then in Deuteronomy 17:17, God gave the a commandment that the king should not multiply wives to himself. Yet David broke these rules.

Second Samuel 13 provides us with a glimpse of even more chaos: "After this Absalom the son of David had a lovely sister, whose name was Tamar; and Amnon the son of David loved her" (verse 1). There was a mixture of the families, and this verse points out a brother and a sister, then a stepbrother, a half-brother, the same father, and another mother. Second Samuel 13:2 says: "Amnon was so distressed over his sister Tamar that he became sick; for she was a virgin. And it was improper for Amnon to do anything to her." He was distressed because he was in love with Tamar. He devised a plot to get Tamar into his bedroom, which he acted out in verse 14. She tried to dissuade him. "However, he would not heed her voice; and being stronger than she, he forced her and lay with her" (verse 14). This family was at dysfunction junction. As the father, David was loose, but his son entered a whole new level of lowness. Amnon raped his half-sister.

While I can't prove what I'm what about to say from this Bible text, I've studied these chapters over and over again. It seems like David never sat down to talk about sex with his children. I don't think he taught them about what was right and what was wrong, nor was there a time when he openly confessed his own shortcomings. He never said, "Yes, I had an affair, and, children, here's the lesson I've learned from that experience and what you ought to learn from it." From what I know about David, this conversation never happened.

Today, surveys show that less than 5 percent of Christian couples provide an honest and thorough explanation about sexuality to their children. Children are smart and intuitive; they have a sensitive antenna with which they pick up on many things. In fact, even at a very young age, they know a great deal more than we give them credit for, yet they will emulate what they see and hear or what they don't see and hear.

How did King David respond to Amnon's horrible action? If you mix relational chaos with a passive parent, then you have a volatile situation. Second Samuel 13:21 says: "When King David heard of all these things, he was very angry." You've just seen David's complete response—he got mad. This reaction falls into David's normal behavior pattern. A few chapters back consider David's reaction to problems. The prophet came to him and said, "Let me tell you about two men: one was rich; one was poor. The rich man had lots of sheep, yet the poor man only had one. When the rich man was hungry, he had a friend over, so he killed the poor man's single lamb and then ate it for dinner." And what was David's response? He got very angry and flew off the handle with his temper. He said, "Kill that man." Really? Kill a man for stealing an animal?

Now, when his daughter was raped, David got mad. Notice the Scriptures don't say that David called in Amnon, nor did he confront Amnon. There was no parental intervention, mature resolution, or godly restitution. The only fact we know for certain is that David was mad about it.

In the middle of this situation, another son, Absalom, the brother of Tamar, was watching his dad's response and asked, "Where's the justice?" When Absalom saw nothing happening, each day his resentment and anger grew. In a bit you will see how this resentment caused Absalom to become a juvenile delinquent.

When Dr. Loren Moshen from the National Institute of Mental Health analyzed the census figures, he found the absence of a father to be a stronger contributing factor than poverty to juvenile delinquency.[2] In the midst of any election, people will talk about this matter, but they say, "The problem is poverty," or "Race is the problem." They are wrong. Dr. Motion is saying, "I've studied it, and absent parenting is a bigger cause than those other factors. The cure for crime isn't in the electric chair but in the high chair."

The root of this problem begins when children are very young. No parent can shirk their responsibilities without consequences. When Socrates spoke to the men of Athens, he marveled that "they could turn over every stone to find wealth for themselves but pay so little care to their children to whom one day they would relinquish all." There aren't any perfect parents, but you can be a good parent. If you want to be a good parent, you can never be passive, aloof, unengaged, or uninvolved.

As Amnon attacked Tamar and King David was passive, with Absalom growing angry, there was someone else watching this whole scene unfold: Solomon, another one of the sons. Later on Solomon would grow up, become the king, and write the Book of Proverbs, which includes instructions about raising children. One of the most famous sayings of King Solomon is found in Proverbs 22:6: "Train up a child in the way he should go, and when he is old he will not depart from it." What does it mean to "train up a child"? It isn't passive, but it involves active engagement. It doesn't mean tossing out a few words of advice every couple of months. The Hebrew word *hanoch* for "train" means "to put something into someone's mouth" or "to affect their taste."

An Arabic word closely associated with *hanoch*, and sounding a lot like it, describes a process in which parents take date honey with their little fingers, then put it on the lips of a newborn. This honey stimulates the sucking reflex for breastfeeding. When Solomon used the phrase "train up a child," he meant to stimulate that child's hunger and thirst for godliness and godly behavior.

Do you play with your child? Do you pray with your child? Are you actively involved to stimulate their desire to be godly? If your little boy says, "I want to be just like Daddy when I grow up," is that a good thing? If the baby girl says, "I want to be just like Mommy," is that a good desire? Are you actively stimulating your children? If so, then you are training them.

In 2 Samuel 13, the story moves from a ruptured home to focus on Absalom, the rebel son. He was watching and had decided to act out against his father's indifference. This boy wanted justice served in response to how his sister Tamar had been treated. Second Samuel 13:28 says: "Now Absalom had commanded his servants, saying, 'Watch now, when Amnon's heart is merry with wine [in other words, "Let's booze this guy up a little bit"], and when I say to you, 'Strike Amnon!' then kill him. Do not be afraid. Have I not commanded you? Be courageous and valiant'" (Words in brackets added.)

Absalom was encouraging his buddies. He was saying, "You are the dispensers of justice. My dad didn't do anything, so you be courageous because this is the right thing to do." As Absalom had commanded, the servants of Absalom killed Amnon. Then the remaining sons of King David each got on their mules and fled.

What was David's reaction to Absalom's actions? Second Samuel 13:36 says: "So it was, as soon as he had finished speaking, that the king's sons indeed came, and they lifted up their voice and wept. Also the king and all his servants wept very bitterly." David's reaction as a grieving father is understandable. Second Samuel 13:37-39 says:

> But Absalom fled and went to Talmai the son of
> Ammihud, king of Geshur. And David mourned
> for his son every day. So Absalom fled and went to
> Geshur, and was there three years. [Now watch this.]
> And King David longed to go to Absalom. For he
> had been comforted concerning Amnon, because he
> was dead. (Words in brackets added.)

From the Bible, we know King David had gotten mad
and then cried, but he never went to confront his son Amnon.
David remained passive and never saw Absalom after he
murdered his brother. Yet notice this verse says: "David
longed to go to Absalom."

Why didn't David go to see Absalom? As the king, David
could do whatever he wanted. I don't know the answer. I
could ask this same question about many family situations.
Why didn't that man humble himself? Why didn't that
woman decide to reconcile with her husband? Why doesn't
that stubborn young man get together with his parents and
talk out this issue? Whatever the family dynamics, we get
used to our usual way of dealing with an issue and refuse to
do whatever it takes to rectify situations. King David's story
is a classic example of how a passive father responded to a
difficult situation.

As I follow the story, I understand this cycle of violence
and immorality because of the unexpressed resentment and
anger. The situation was perpetuated and then amplified.
Why? This situation was perpetuated because of a passive
and absent father.

Charles Colson of Prison Fellowship said, "Take away
the family, and you might as well build prison cells right
now." Why does this happen when you take away the family?
An incredible insecurity gets set up in the psyche of a young

man or woman as a result of the lack of masculine leadership in the home. Dr. James Dobson writes: "The Western world stands at a great crossroads in its history. It is my opinion that our very survival as a people will depend on the presence or absence of masculine leadership in the home."

Over the last thirty years from 1980 up to today, there has been a rise in violent crime among our nation's youth. This corresponds with the increase in fathers who have abandoned their families. Teenage aggression and hostility mirrors the growth of single-parent families. Research shows the rise of violent crimes commited by youthful offenders in various states with first, Mississippi at 48 percent; second, Louisiana at 45 percent; and third, New Mexico at 37 percent. This situation isn't a theory, but our reality.[3]

The young man Absalom killed his stepbrother and then ran away. But if you look at 2 Samuel 15, you can see his violence turn into subversion and his behavior become even more erratic. In chapter 15, Absalom returned to Jerusalem, took fifty young men with him, and went out to the gates of the city. As each person came into the city:

> Absalom would say to him, "Look, your case is good and right; but there is no deputy of the king to hear you." Moreover Absalom would say, "Oh, that I were made judge in the land, and everyone who has any suit or cause would come to me; then I would give him justice." [This young man is a perfect politician!] And so it was, whenever anyone came near to bow down to him, that he would put out his hand and take him and kiss him. [See how he mounts his campaign?] In this manner Absalom acted toward all Israel who came to the king for judgment. [Watch what happens.]

So Absalom stole the hearts of the men of Israel.
(2 Samuel 14:23-24; words in brackets added.)

As Absalom talked with the people at the city gate, he started a coup. This young man was trying to get his dad's attention. Don't miss that the stability of the entire nation of Israel rested on the single relationship between a father and a son. And this nation was about to split.

The focus of the story returns to King David as a remorseful father at the heart of this chapter. There are two principal reasons for the dysfunction or breakdown in the family of David. First, there was proximity without intimacy. There was physical closeness, but each person was emotionally detached. In 2 Samuel 13, we read that Absalom fled and was gone for three years. David's general and friend, Joab, knew this situation with Absalom was eating David up, yet the king wouldn't swallow his pride to go and get him. Joab created a plan to bring Absalom back to town, and then begged David to see him. The king said, "Okay, bring him." Second Samuel 14:23-24 says: "So Joab arose and went to Geshur, and brought Absalom to Jerusalem. [This sounds like the situation with Absalom is moving toward resolution, right?] And the king said, 'Let him return to his own house, but do not let him see my face.' [Ouch!] So Absalom returned to his own house, but did not see the king's face." (Words in brackets added.) Second Samuel 14:28 says: "Absalom dwelt two full years in Jerusalem, but did not see the king's face." The son had proximity without intimacy with his father. Healing wasn't possible unless Absalom could see his father.

His proximity without intimacy turned into resentment:

Therefore Absalom sent for Joab, to send him to the king, but he would not come to him. And when he sent again the second time, he would not come. So he said to his servants, "See, Joab's field is near mine, and he has barley there; go and set it on fire." And Absalom's servants set the field on fire. Then Joab arose and came to Absalom's house, and said to him, "Why have your servants set my field on fire?" And Absalom answered Joab, "Look, I sent to you, saying, 'Come here, so that I may send you to the king, to say, "Why have I come from Geshur? It would be better for me to be there still."' Now therefore, let me see the king's face; but if there is iniquity in me, let him execute me." (2 Samuel 14:29-32)

Just as David longed to see Absalom, Absalom had longed to see David, yet the king had forbidden it. Because of this proximity without intimacy, Absalom grew resentful.

Back in the 1800s, there was a notable busy politician named Charles Francis Adams who kept a journal. One day his journal entry said, "Went fishing with my son today. A day wasted."

Adams's son also kept a journal, and on this same day he wrote, "Went fishing with my dad today—the most wonderful day of my life." Here's another example of proximity without intimacy. While the son and father were in the same boat, they were not on the same page. Fathers, it's much easier to build a boy than to repair a man. And how do you build a boy or a girl? You sow time and intimacy into their lives through your proximity.

Gallup polled a thousand teenagers and learned that during a twenty-four-hour test period, 42 percent of them had not received any words of praise. Half of them had not received a hug or a kiss, and 44 percent had never heard the words, "I love you."

Some of you may be thinking, *Well, they don't need to hear it again because I've already told them enough.* We need to tell our children that we love them each day—in fact, several times a day. If you talk with them on the phone tell them, "I love you." Our families need to be buttressed, built up, and fortified in that love.

While proximity without intimacy was the first cause of King David's family dysfunction, there was something else. The family also had dissension without resolution. This longtime rift between David and Absalom had never been resolved. Absalom killed his brother and then set on fire the fields of General Joab. Finally in 2 Samuel 15, he started a coup to get his father's attention.

What happened? Historically, we know Absalom was successful in his subversion and managed to split the nation. In fact, Absalom inaugurated himself as the king in 2 Samuel 15 through 18. King Absalom rallied a whole group of people against King David. He managed to kick King David out of Jerusalem; his father had to flee like a refugee. The family conflict had actually created two armies: the army of King David and the army of King Absalom, which were fighting each other. It amounted to a family feud on steroids.

Let's turn to 2 Samuel 18. David's army was about to face Absalom in battle. Second Samuel 18:5 described the briefing before the battle: "Now the king had commanded Joab, Abishai, and Ittai, saying, 'Deal gently for my sake with the young man Absalom.' [Notice that David wouldn't talk to Absalom or resolve his conflict, and yet he instructed them, "Deal gently with him."] And all the people heard when the king gave all the captains orders concerning Absalom." (Words in brackets added.)

David was only thinking about his son. During the battle, Absalom was killed, and a runner came with the news that

David and his army had won the war. Second Samuel 18:28-29 says: "So Ahimaaz called out and said to the king, 'All is well!' And he bowed down with his face to the earth before the king, and said, 'Blessed be the LORD your God, who has delivered up the men who raised their hand against my lord the king!' [Most kings would rejoice at such news, but watch how David responded.] The king said, 'Is the young man Absalom safe?'" (Words in brackets added.) In the middle of a national war, the king was thinking about his son. He wasn't focused on the battle nor thinking, *I hope I get to Jerusalem by the end of the month. I hope I get my throne back.* King David's mind was focused on his son.

For two years, Absalom was in Jerusalem, yet his father, David, never went to him. Why didn't he? I don't know. In the same way, I don't understand what dysfunction was set up in your family, but I do know that if you're a mom or a dad and there is a rift in your family, you should do whatever it takes to reach out and resolve the conflict. Or, if you're a son or a daughter and you've been hurt by your parents, don't sit there and say, "Well, I'm just going to wait for them to call." Instead, *you* reach out and call them and tell them that you love them.

You may be protesting, saying, "Me? Why should *I* reach out since *they* blew it?" That may be true, but the last time I checked, one of the Ten Commandments concerned honoring your father and your mother. It is still in the Bible. Here's another consideration: Jesus Christ has forgiven you, and God has given you His unconditional love. Don't you think that people who have received unconditional love should give unconditional love? In fact, the only ones equipped to show unconditional love are those who have received unconditional love. As a Christian, you have a different standard—and a different power—so go and heal your relationship.

I want to conclude this chapter with 2 Samuel 18:33, which says: "The king was deeply moved, and went up to the chamber over the gate, and wept. And as he went, he said thus: 'O my son Absalom—my son, my son Absalom—if only I had died in your place! O Absalom my son, my son!'" King David's reaction was too little, too late. He should have used these same words in speaking to Absalom two years earlier when his son was in Jerusalem, or three years earlier when Absalom was in Geshur. David had the opportunity— he even longed to go see him. But David couldn't resolve anything now because Absalom was dead.

I've seen an almost exact replay of this Bible story in the lives of families I meet in emergency rooms and hospitals. I have even watched a situation take place in my own family. My father was very aloof and proud. My brother had a long-standing rift with my dad, and neither one of them would budge. I even watched them have a fistfight once in our own home. You talk about a traumatic situation for a young teenager to watch, but the rift was that strong in my family. The rift grew and grew until the night my father called me on the phone. I had never heard such grief in anyone's voice until he announced, "Your brother's been killed in a motorcycle accident."

All of us were grieved and torn up about my brother's death, but it absolutely crippled my father. For the rest of his life, everything was filtered through that emotional failure to reconnect with his son.

Now you may be thinking, *Great. I'm reading this chapter to get depressed.* I've used this chapter to frame the problem in today's family. But in the following chapters, the Scriptures will provide solutions. Thank God that Isaiah

59:19 says: "When the enemy comes in like a flood, the Spirit of the LORD will lift up a standard against him."

There are ways to secure your families, your relationships, and the next generation. The first principle is communication. As a family, learn to communicate. The Church has many resources to help you do that. Because, parents, how you communicate with your children is setting the pattern for how they will communicate with their children and grandchildren in the future. Your children are going to copy what you do.

The second principle is to humble yourself. Bring your family together and begin with these sentences: "I'm sorry for_____." Don't use something like, "I have a few things I want to point out to you." Instead begin with "I'm sorry for_____," then "Forgive me for_____." As you use these words, you're helping your children develop the aability to practice humility in their future.

For the third principle, I want you to think outside the normal idea of your own family. Consider the larger world, in which there are millions of children who are street kids. What will you do about them? Can you get involved in mentorship or Big Brother or Big Sister programs? Have you ever considered adoption?

These kids are abandoned, but if they could be brought into a Christian home, or if a Christian could reach out to them once a week, or become a mentor such as a Big Brother or a Big Sister, it would change lives. What do the statistics prove? Yes, the family statistics are bad, but they improve if there's a mentor or a Big Brother or Big Sister in the picture. Crime drops, absenteeism at school goes down, and drug usage decreases when a child interacts with a loving, positive Big Brother or Big Sister.

While there are no perfect parents or perfect families or perfect homes, you can have and should have a secure home. I once received a note from a little girl who wrote, "My dad says I'm enormously gorgeous." Isn't that a great phrase? She continued, "I wonder if I really am. To be enormously gorgeous, Sarah says you need to have beautiful, long curly hair like she has. I don't. To be enormously gorgeous, Justin says you must have perfectly straight white teeth like he has. I don't. To be enormously gorgeous, Jessica says you can't have any of those little brown dots on your face called freckles. I do. To be enormously gorgeous, Mark says you have to be the smartest kid in the seventh-grade class. I'm not. To be enormously gorgeous, Steven says you have to be able to tell the funniest jokes in the school. I don't. To be enormously gorgeous, Loren says you need to live in the nicest neighborhood in town and in the prettiest house, and I don't. To be enormously gorgeous, Matthew says you can only wear the coolest clothes and the most popular shoes. I don't. To be enormously gorgeous, Samantha says you need to come from a perfect family, and I don't. But every night at bedtime, my dad gives me a big hug and says, 'You are enormously gorgeous, and I love you.' Hmm, my dad must know something my friends don't."

I hope that you know something nobody else knows. When your children wake you up at 1 A.M., then 3 A.M., then 5 A.M., it is a gift. Your children are all gifts from God. Your children don't have the equipment to deal with life like you do. The choice is yours. You don't have to be perfect or flawless and never make mistakes. Instead, try to do your part to communicate, humble yourself, and help shape those precious children.

Chapter 5

STOP THE DOMINOES

I don't play dominoes. In fact, I'm not an "indoor game" person because I like to get up and move around. If I make a move in a game, I'll then go to another room and do something else and come back in time for my next move. And I don't quite understand the game of dominoes, but this week I found out there's an International Federation of Dominoes.

Not only is there an International Federation of Dominoes, but there's a whole group into domino-toppling. They set dominoes up on their edges, and as they fall down, they hit each other and topple over. Throughout the world, people try each year to outdo the last record. Various associations of domino-topplers play on several different continents and in many different countries. In November of 2006 in Holland, they set a world record when about 4,400,000 dominoes were set up and fell in a single topple.

As I was reading this, I thought, *There are a lot of people with way too much time on their hands!* These games are where we get the phrase the "domino effect." Like dominoes that hit each other and topple down, the domino effect is when small occurrences add up to a chain of events that ultimately erupts into a catastrophe. In this chapter, I'm speaking principally of the domino effect in families. As I discussed in the last chapter, absent or passive parents can create a devastating domino effect in families.

As I was preparing for this chapter, I found this phrase, "domino effect," came up time and time again. For example, Terrence Holmes, who wrote a paper for Johnson-Smith University, said, "The domino effect is that fathers are vanishing from families. Unattached males are the cause of many of today's social ills." I also read a book review of *Pearls of Wisdom: Surviving Against All Odds* by Marie Davis, which recounts the stories of five different women who experienced abuse, abandonment, or neglect in the home. The reviewer wrote about the common threads in these stories and how the domino effect can throw a life out of control. I also read a magazine article, "Resolving Child Support in America," which addressed the matter of a father's absence in a home. It said, "By fixing this problem, you're fixing the major problem, which has caused a domino effect in the world."

Here's my question: How do you stop the domino effect? How do you prevent this chain reaction from breaking hearts, ruining families, and devastating relationships? To find one answer, I returned to the game of dominos. I asked, how do you stop a line of real dominoes from falling during a domino-toppling contest? The experts will tell you that it's all about position and placement. If you don't place the dominoes close enough or you place them at the wrong angle, they won't fall and you won't break the record. The key is placement and movement.

In this chapter, I want to discuss where we place our lives and the moves we make. Can we angle, or incline, our hearts in the right direction to stop the fall of these dominoes? I have positive news for you. Through research, a Christian businessman's committee found that when the father is an active believer, there is about a 75 percent likelihood the children will also become active believers. Your first step as a father or a mother is to fall madly in love with Jesus Christ and obey Him. The dominoes can be stopped! Our answer for stopping the dominoes comes from Joshua 24:14-15. Joshua said to the people: "Now therefore, fear the LORD, serve Him in sincerity and in truth, and put away the gods which your fathers served on the other side of the River and in Egypt. Serve the LORD! And if it seems evil to you to serve the LORD, choose for yourselves this day whom you will serve, whether the gods which your fathers served that were on the other side of the River, or the gods of the Amorites, in whose land you dwell. But as for me and my house, we will serve the LORD."

In Joshua's day, the domino effect was already in place, but this man took a stand to stop it. How did he do it? It took a strong man, with a straight message, at a strategic moment. Joshua took this public stance in Joshua 24.

As the leader of the nation of Israel, Joshua issued a challenge to the people, and then he made his own personal choice. First, let's look at Joshua as the general and head of the Israelite military. Earlier in his life, Joshua had been Moses' assistant. When Moses died and Joshua took over the leadership, he was about eighty years old. At this point, in Joshua 24, Joshua was probably about 100 years old, and because of his twenty years of leadership, he has earned the right for the people to listen to him.

This book addresses the issues of homeland security. Joshua was the head of homeland security in Israel. In his younger days, Joshua had been one of the original spies

Moses had sent to check out the land. He was one of two spies who, in faith, brought a positive report about the land. Now in Joshua 24, this aging leader has gathered the people at a place called Shechem, a very important place in Bible history. At Shechem, Abraham had built an altar to dedicate his life to God. Jacob recommitted his life to God at Shechem.

In this historical place, Joshua gathered the people to address the nation. Notice Joshua didn't speak as the chairman of the nation, the general of the armed forces of Israel, or as a political leader; he addressed them as the leader of his *home*, saying, "As for me and my house." The word for "house" in Hebrew is *bite* and means "household" or "family." Why did Joshua make this emphasis? He could have said, "I'm commanding you as the head of this nation," or "As your political and military leader …" Instead, Joshua spoke as the head of a family—because he knew the moral temperature of the nation was set in the home. The family was going to either strengthen or weaken any nation, including Israel. If the family was strong, then the nation would be strong, but if the family was weak, then the nation would be weak. If your family unraveled, then you could unravel your nation, and Joshua knew it.

Recently I read about a brilliant entrepreneur in Japan who saw a need in his culture for lonely people, especially elderly parents and grandparents whose kids and grandkids wouldn't visit them. He created a special service where, for a fee of 150,000 yen, or about $1,400, he would provide three trained "surrogate" family members to spend three hours at their homes. You may wonder if he had any business, but in fact, there's a waiting list. For this rent-a-family enterprise, hired actors play the roles of children, grandchildren, daughters, and sons-in-law. They usually sit around and talk, but often the client berates their pretend children for leaving them alone and sad.

Why has this unusual scheme caught on? Mr. Cararu Inuwae said, "There are many old people who feel sad because everyone is chasing money and no one is paying attention to the human spirit." The moral of this story is that the rat race is a lonely place. When material possessions come at the expense of meaningful relationships, they create a lonely environment. Mr. Inuwae continued, "I have a whole culture that has developed that way of thinking."

In Joshua 24, this general, civic leader, and family man was taking a stand. Joshua 24:14 says: "Therefore, fear the LORD, serve Him in sincerity and in truth, and put away [foreign] gods." One commentator said, "The language that Joshua is using here in this chapter indicates the people already are having a hankering toward idolatry." They were already leaning toward it. With idolatry, the cultural dominoes were starting to topple, and it explains why Joshua made this kind of a stand. By the way, this message marks Joshua's last stand and his final state-of-the-union address.

Let's look at Joshua's challenge to the people in greater detail to learn how to stop the dominoes. The first step is you need to *choose*. In Joshua 24:15, the seasoned leader said: "Choose for yourselves this day whom you will serve." Now look at the previous verse, verse 14. Joshua said: "Now therefore...." If you study the Bible much, you will notice there's a rule in place here: Every time there's a "therefore," you find out what it's "there for." No one begins a thought with the word *therefore*; it's always attached to something else that has been said. In this passage, General Joshua reached back into the history of the Jewish people. For four hundred years, God had faithfully raised up a nation, delivered them from bondage, and brought them into the

Promised Land. Now God was preparing them to make a choice on this very day.

Let's return to Joshua 24:

Then Joshua gathered all the tribes of Israel to Shechem and called for the elders of Israel, for their heads, for their judges, and for their officers; and they presented themselves before God. And Joshua said to all the people, "Thus says the LORD God of Israel: 'Your fathers, including Terah, the father of Abraham and the father of Nahor, dwelt on the other side of the River [that's the Euphrates, which is in today's Iraq, by the way] in old times; and they served other gods. Then I took your father Abraham from the other side of the River, led him throughout all the land of Canaan, and multiplied his descendants and gave him Isaac. To Isaac I gave Jacob and Esau. To Esau I gave the mountains of Seir to possess, but Jacob and his children went down to Egypt. Also I sent Moses and Aaron, and I plagued Egypt, according to what I did among them. Afterward I brought you out. Then I brought your fathers out of Egypt, and you came to the sea; and the Egyptians pursued your fathers with chariots and horsemen to the Red Sea. So they cried out to the LORD; and He put darkness between you and the Egyptians, brought the sea upon them, and covered them. And your eyes saw what I did in Egypt. Then you dwelt in the wilderness a long time. And I brought you into the land of the Amorites, who dwelt on the other side of the Jordan, and they fought with you. But I gave them into your hand, that you might possess their land, and I destroyed them from before you. Then Balak, the son of Zippor, king of Moab, arose to make war against Israel, and sent and called Balaam the son of Beor to curse you. But I would not listen to Balaam; therefore he continued to bless you. So I delivered you out of his hand. Then you went over the Jordan and came to Jericho. And the men of Jericho fought against you—also the Amorites, the Perizzites, the Canaanites.... But I delivered them into your hand. I sent the hornet before you which drove them out from before you, also the two kings of the Amorites, but not with your sword or with your bow. I have given you a land for which you did not labor, and cities which you did not build, and you dwell in them; you eat of the vineyards and olive groves which you did not plant.' Now therefore...." (Verses 1-14; words in brackets added.)

I want you to see this connection: Joshua was saying, "Look, Israel, this is all that God has done in four hundred years of history. He raised you up, He delivered you; you didn't do anything, He brought you here. And He brought you here today to make a choice. Choose this day whom you will serve."

As I read this passage, I can't help but think that perhaps God has brought us here for the same occasion. The Lord wants us to make a choice that could change our families and even the next generation. God wants us to heal and reconcile broken relationships that have been beaten up and bruised for a long time. The change process begins as you choose whom you will serve.

By the way, each time you hear a message or read a book like *Homeland Security*, it should bring you to a place where you make yet another choice about whatever it is you are studying or hearing. Without this choice, you don't grow. But when you come to a place to change your behavior based on what you read or hear, that's when you begin to discover real growth. You have to make careful choices because once you make them, as the old saying goes, "Your choices turn around and make you."

Let's notice the specific choice Joshua told the people to make in Joshua 24:14. He said: "Fear the LORD, serve Him in sincerity and in truth." If someone "fears the LORD," it means they have honor and respect for the Lord. This action begins with a personal commitment to God and God's standard of truth for your life, for your business, and for your family. Have you ever stated this intention for your family directly to them?

Joshua was standing in front of the whole country, and his family probably was there to hear his declaration: "As for me and my house, we're going to serve the Lord." I encourage you to declare a purpose statement for your family, such as, "Kids, sweetheart, we're going to serve the Lord." I admire that Joshua clearly stated his intention.

Last week, I was talking with John Fuller. You may recognize his name because John is the cohost, along with Dr. James Dobson, of the *Focus on the Family* radio broadcast. Each day John and Dr. Dobson are in the studio talking about a number of issues. When I talked with John, I asked him several questions.

First, I wanted to know about his family situation. He told me that he has six children, with five at home and one attending college. I said, "You go home every night to five kids. After hearing about all of the alarming trends from the *Focus on the Family* guests day after day, week after week, month after month, what does that do to you when you go home to your kids?"

Right off the bat, John said, "It makes my parenting more intentional." For a moment, let's consider this concept of intentional parenting that honors God. Austin L. Sorensen once said, "A child is not likely to find a father in God unless he finds something of God in his father." When you make a decision with your family to serve the Lord, that's intentional parenting.

Let me tell you, whenever you come to the point that you say, "Tonight I'm going to make a clear choice to honor God," then you're going to find all of Heaven on your side. Suddenly you have all of God's resources, including the Holy Spirit's power, at your disposal, because that's exactly what God wants. And the quickest way to become a partner with God is to choose to honor God with your family.

Psalm 127:1 says: "Unless the LORD builds the house, they labor in vain who build it." This assignment can't be completed on your own by saying, "Okay, here goes. I'm going to do this because it's really all about me."

No, it's not about you. You need help and strength far beyond your own ability—you need the Lord's strength in your life. When you say, "My purpose or my choice is to honor God," then the Lord will partner with you.

I want to make a second observation from Joshua 24:14-15. We need to separate ourselves from any idols we might have. Notice Joshua said to put away the gods their fathers had served. He was telling the Jewish people to put away their idols.

You may be thinking, *This verse has nothing to do with my life. I don't have any false gods or images in my house.* While you may not have any literal, physical images in your house, do you understand the spiritual meaning of an *idol?* An idol could be an ideology or a desire. Anything that replaces God is an idol.

What are the priorities in your life? Your answer will determine if you have an idol or not. However you answer, here's a news flash: Your kids already know your priorities whether you verbalize them or not. They know by watching your life because they can see if what you say and what you do are the same.

As Joshua said, each of you needs to put away the gods your fathers served. In today's context, you must put away the baggage that you got from your parents. I've heard people say things like, "I am the way I am because my dad did this," or, "My mom did that, so I do it, too." Whatever you have experienced is legitimate, but if you know the reason you do what you do, you can change because you have the Holy Spirit living in you.

Guess what? You can *choose* to change. When you know what your issues are, with the Holy Spirit's help, you can face them and make a change in your life.

You may protest, saying, "I'm angry because I've got that hot Latino blood." Or, "I'm Italian." Or, "I'm Irish." You can say something about any people group. The truth is, you are angry because you are a fallen human being. All of us have those propensities. Do not excuse your behavior. Put away those sinful actions and leave them behind.

Let's return to the dominoes. How do you stop them from falling? It's all about placement, movement, and angle. Move anything out of your life if it needs to change. Frankly, in this culture, many of us need to rid ourselves of the dogged pursuit of material possessions. We make materialism our highest goal while precious relationships are being cast aside all around us.

Imagine what it would mean to your kids if you were to sit them down and say, "Kids, I want you to know Dad's career isn't going to be the most important thing any longer"

Or, "Dad's hobbies or Mom's hobbies or our careers aren't going to be the most important things any longer."

Instead, you tell them, "From now on, God is going to be the most important aspect of our lives." Then you tell them, "I'm going to love God, I'm going to love you, and we're going to love God together." Your changed life would mean a lot.

To stop the dominoes, you need to choose and you need to separate. Why? Because it works. When you choose whom you're going to serve and the standard of truth that is going to govern your life, you separate from anything that would hold up that choice. This change works in the next generation and the next and the next.

In the previous chapter, I listed a number of negative statistics about what occurs in fatherless families. Here are a few statistics about what happens in families with fathers. In 1958, researchers studied seventeen thousand children born in the UK (England), following up with each one at age seven, at age eleven, at age sixteen, at age twenty-three, and at age thirty-three. They discovered that children with an involved dad had less emotional and behavioral difficulties when they reached their adolescent years. This same study concluded that teenagers who felt close to their dads in adolescence would live more contented, satisfying adult marital lives, and their relationships would be more rewarding. Finally, this study revealed that girls with strong relationships with their fathers in adolescence had less psychological distress than other adults. These statistics show the domino effect *can* be stopped.

Another study over a twenty-six-year period considered the same group of 379 people. Researchers found the single most important childhood factor in developing empathy is parental involvement. Do you want to raise a generation that cares about people? If you care for your children while they're being raised, then they will care for others. Many of you might be thinking, *You don't have a clue about what's going on in my house. Do you know how much time my kids spend doing other things?*

I'm glad you brought up this topic. Here's a *USA Today* study about where most teens spend their time: "The average number of hours per week boys and girls say they spend surfing the Internet, 16 hours a week; writing e-mail, 17 hours a week (Who are they emailing? Do you know?); working at a job, 8 to 10 hours a week; doing homework, 8 to 12 hours a week; exercising, 6 to 7 hours a week; and volunteering, 3 to 4 hours a week."[1]

You may be thinking, *See, here's the reason we're not involved. That's the problem. They're just too busy, and I'm too busy.* But wait a minute—you haven't heard the rest of the story. They asked these children to complete this sentence: "If I could, I would spend more time doing ____." Notice their answers: Nine percent said they would spend the time studying; 17 percent said they'd spend more time at a paying job. Twenty-two percent said they'd spend more time working out; 44 percent said they would spend more time with friends; and *50 percent* of these students said they'd spend more time with their families.

Why aren't they spending time with their families? Again, as I said in the previous chapter, I don't know why David didn't go see Absalom. Nor do I understand why Absalom was not permitted to see David. But whatever those dynamics and whoever had to take the initiative, it just wasn't taken. But all of the research shows us that today the dominoes can be stopped.

I want to conclude this chapter by returning to Joshua's choice concerning his own family. This aging general made a personal as well as a collective choice when he said: "As for me and my house, we will serve the LORD." If I were to paraphrase it, Joshua said, "Look, I can't speak for you, and I can't speak for the whole nation. I can't tell you what choice you're going to make. But I want to tell you what choice *I'm* going to make. *I'm* going to serve God with all my heart. And I'm going to serve my family and serve the Lord with my family. My wife and my children are going to see that in my life."

Here's the principle: Our personal spiritual commitment should affect every relationship in our lives. Hudson Taylor once said, "If your father, your mother, your sister, your brother, even the cat and dog in your very house isn't happier for you being a Christian, there's a question as to whether you really are."

You will not have the perfect family, because there is no perfect family. Every family tree has to have some sap, right? Someone once said, "The problem with being a parent is that once you're experienced, you're unemployed."

Joshua was operating from a relational template that he received from the man who used to be his boss, Moses. Throughout Joshua's life, he heard Moses, he served Moses, and he was Moses' assistant. He heard the instruction of the Law, and exactly what Moses said he should do, he did. In Deuteronomy 6, Moses spoke the Word of God to the people:

> Now this is the commandment, and these are the statutes and judgments which the LORD your God has commanded to teach you, that you may observe them in the land which you are crossing over to possess, that you may fear [or honor, or respect, or reverence] the LORD your God, to keep all His statutes and His commandments which I command you, you and your

son and your grandson, all the days of your life, and that your days may be prolonged. Therefore hear, O Israel, and be careful to observe it, that it may be well with you, and that you may multiply greatly as the LORD God of your fathers has promised you— "a land flowing with milk and honey." (Verses 1-3; words in brackets are added.)

The people were to respond to God in two different ways: personally and collectively. This was exactly how Joshua responded. Deuteronomy 6:5-6 says: "You shall love the LORD your God with all your heart, with all your soul, and with all your strength. And these words which I command you today shall be in your heart." These verses highlight the personal commitment we are to make to God's truth.

Deuteronomy 6:7 says: "You shall teach them diligently to your children, and shall talk of them when you sit in your house, when you walk by the way, when you lie down, and when you rise up." This verse highlights the collective, communal choice we are to make, to place God in the center of our homes.

Finally, Deuteronomy 6:20-24 says:

When your son asks you in time to come [and boy, your children will have a way of asking a lot of questions!], saying, "What is the meaning of the testimonies, the statutes, and the judgments which the LORD our God has commanded you?" then you shall say to your son: "We were slaves of Pharaoh in Egypt, and the LORD brought us out of Egypt with a mighty hand; and the LORD showed signs and wonders before our eyes, great and severe, against Egypt, Pharaoh, and all his household. Then He brought us out from there, that He might bring us in, to give us the land of which He swore to our fathers. And the LORD commanded us to observe all these statutes, to fear the LORD our God, for our good always, that He might preserve us alive, as it is this day." (Words in brackets added.)

Joshua followed Moses' exact instructions. These verses gave the Jewish people the model, or template, that everyone was supposed to follow when they entered the land. These verses provide us today with God's pattern for passing on truth to the next generation. Parents are to pass it along to their children so the next generation can be equipped to do the same, parent to child; so that generation can be equipped the same, parent to child. If you want to tip any dominoes, those truths are the ones you want to tip. Parent to child: truth, sincerity. Parent to child: truth, sincerity. On to the next generation: your son, your grandson, all the way down.

To me, these words of Billy Sunday are unforgettable: "The great tragedy of my life is I've led thousands of people to Christ, and my own sons are not saved." Those words are from a heartbroken father who wanted to pass truth on to the next generation. The parent is a partner with God in making disciples of children.

When we dedicate our children to the Lord, or you dedicate yourself to the Lord, is your house a place of sincerity and truth, as it was for Joshua? Is God the center of your life? Intentional parenting honors the Lord. Did you know that toymakers watch the divorce rate? Why? They know that when the divorce rate goes up, toy sales skyrocket. When there's a breakup in a home, there's an abandonment issue because a mom or a dad is leaving and the kids are in the wake. And now with two sets of parents and four sets of grandparents, the adults will often buy more toys in an attempt to win the affections of the child. Yet the children don't want more toys; they simply want more of their parents.

How do you stop the dominoes? You make a choice today. You push out your old life and bring in your relationship with God. You can do it in your community. Put God first in your life, in your home, and let your family see that. Separate from the past, get your children involved in the Church, let them know that you're into God's priorities. We want secure homes in America. We are afraid of the terrorist attacks on all fronts, but we want security in our homes and in our relationships first. Everything we've seen, from biblical examples to secular examples, shows us that the dominoes can be stopped. I pray that you put your stake down and choose for yourself and for your family—however small, however big—to serve the Lord.

Chapter 6

HOW TO PREVENT SOUL THIEVES

Do you remember that anticipation when you waited to bring your first child home from the hospital after their birth? Chuck Swindoll writes this: "Remember waiting for that first baby—the anticipation of bringing home this soft, cuddly, wonderful, delightful infant? And finally the birth and everything's fine and a day or so later you come home. The first week you realize that what you really have is cross between "The Terminator" and "The Swamp Thing." I mean, this creature sleeps when you're awake and is wide awake when you're asleep, and has a set of lungs to drown out a Concord jet. My wife used to say, 'Honey, I'm forgetting what our baby's face looks like, I'm spending so much time at the other end.'"

In this chapter, I'd like to discuss how you can deal with the "right end" of your life, or how to protect your soul and the souls of your family members. I will not break down the debate as to whether man is a bipartite being (having a body and soul) or a tripartite being (having a body, soul, and spirit). While that's a great theological discussion, it would be fun for another study. In these pages, I'm simply going to talk about the inner part of you that the Bible calls the soul.

This week I asked a builder, "What is the average cost of a home security system?"

He said, "People will spend about a thousand dollars per home on a home security system. From that base price, it can go down or it can go way up." A home security system will protect your possessions, but it won't secure your soul. How do you protect your soul? What activities, practices, sights, and sounds are getting into your home and breaking it down?

For a glimpse at where we are today in this area, listen to this study. Thirty years ago, researchers from Johns Hopkins University reported that the greatest fears of grade-school children were 1) animals; 2) being in a dark room; 3) high places; 4) strangers; and 5) loud noises. Things have certainly changed. Today's grade-school children are afraid of: 1) divorce; 2) nuclear war; 3) cancer; 4) pollution; and 5) being mugged.[1]

Admittedly, there are other things that children should fear, but they seem to be unaware of these factors. For example, technology has brought the world into our homes, onto our laptops, and into our phones. You can go anywhere and see anything with the mere touch of a button. I'm sure you've heard of the website called YouTube. During the first year YouTube was on the Internet, the cumulative amount of time people watched it was 9,305 years! What an influence such websites have on our society!

In this chapter I want to refer to Nehemiah 1. I want us to look through the lens of Nehemiah and learn how he brought protection to those who were vulnerable. After church one Sunday in February 2009, I went home and watched the Super Bowl. To some people that's like going to church after church, right? But in the fourth quarter of the game, our TV cable went out! A whole corridor of my community lost reception, and I didn't even bother calling the cable company because I knew their phone system would be jammed. Instead, I waited, and the cable came on just in time to see the end of the game in which the underdog, the New York Giants, defeated the previously unbeaten New England Patriots. My lost reception is not usually the problem. Instead most of us receive too much information through cable television.

Nehemiah understood that Jerusalem needed protection, that it was vulnerable. Its gates needed to be guarded, and its walls needed repair. Today, I suggest we follow the same approach with our own souls and with the souls of our families. We need to set up gatekeepers and watchmen to make sure our families' souls are protected.

Someone once said, "There are three kinds of people: those who make things happen, those who watch things happen, and those who have no idea what's happening."[2] Many people fall into this last camp. They remain unaware of what's going on around them until it's too late. The prophet Nehemiah was firmly in the first category, because based on what he understood, he was going to make things happen. To prevent soul thieves, first you need to ask the right questions; then you need to have the right reaction; and finally, you need to take the right action.

In Nehemiah 1 the prophet had a question:

The words of Nehemiah the son of Hachaliah. It came to pass in the month of Chislev, in the twentieth year, as I was in Shushan the citadel [in modern-day Iraq; Persia in ancient times], that Hanani one of my brethren came with men from Judah; and I asked them concerning the Jews who had escaped, who had survived the captivity, and concerning Jerusalem. And they said to me, "The survivors who are left from the captivity in the province are there in great distress and reproach. The wall of Jerusalem is also broken down, and its gates are burned with fire." (Verses 1-3; words in brackets added.)

Nehemiah was a Jewish captive who lived in Persia. Years before the Babylonian captivity occurred, the Persians had taken over the world. In the palace of their central city of Shushan lived this Jewish man named Nehemiah. Nehemiah 1:11 tells us that he was the cupbearer to the king. You may think of a cupbearer as a type of busboy like we have in our restaurants. Yet in that time period, the cupbearer held a position of high prominence and importance. In the Persian court, the cupbearer equaled the head of homeland security for the whole palace. Nothing, including documents, food, or drink, came into the presence of the king unless it went through the cupbearer first, because they feared someone might try to kill the king. The cupbearer tasted the wine and food before it reached the king. According to historians, only the king's wife was closer to a Persian king than the cupbearer.

In this prominent position, Nehemiah probably had a great life; that is, until one day when a group of people came from Jerusalem and Nehemiah became concerned. He wondered, *What is happening in Jerusalem? These people have returned from captivity. What is it like in that once-devastated city? What is their security situation?* Because Nehemiah was in charge of the palace security, it's natural he would want to know that. But why should Nehemiah even care? After all, he was in a great position in a palace 540 miles from Jerusalem.

There's an old saying, "The Jew never forgets Jerusalem." The heart of God's program on Earth is directed toward Jerusalem, and the Jew knows this, no matter where he or she is living. In Psalm 137:5-6, the psalmist wrote: "If I forget you, O Jerusalem, let my right hand forget its skill! If I do not remember you, let my tongue cling to the roof of my mouth—if I do not exalt Jerusalem above my chief joy." Because Nehemiah was concerned about the homeland and the city of God's program, he asked questions.

Some people don't ask questions because they don't want the information. Some people prefer not to know. They say, "Don't tell me that. I don't want to know those things." Why? Because once you have the information, you might be obligated to do something about it. Instead, Nehemiah wanted to know, and he asked the right questions.

One time a college professor noticed one of his students who seemed lethargic. The professor said, "Young man, what is the biggest problem in America today: ignorance or apathy?"

The student said, "I don't know and I don't care."

Many people live with this type of attitude, but not Nehemiah. He wanted to know, and he cared about what he found out.

In a short article about the vice president of the United States, he was quoted: "The first thing the president and I do every morning is to receive and read intelligence briefings telling of the security threats (plural) that are accumulating against the United States, of the terrorist groups that are in sixty different countries."

Wouldn't that be difficult information to get immediately when you wake up—to learn the specifics about groups in sixty countries that want nothing more than to attack your homeland and way of life? When I read that article, I thought,

That's what we need. We need intelligence briefings to warn us about the security threats against our own homes. Like those people in Jerusalem at the time of Nehemiah, many people need to be set free from their captivity to sin, and they are in great danger.

Also notice what Nehemiah learned about the conditions in Jerusalem. The Scripture says, "The survivors there are in great distress" (verse 3). Then he continued and described the city: "The wall is broken down, the gates have been burned with fire" (verse 3). History records that in 586 B.C., King Nebuchadnezzar from Babylon attacked Jerusalem, put holes in the walls, breached them, went into the city, burned it down, and destroyed its gates. Nehemiah heard that the city was still in that condition. Did you catch the interesting description of the people living in Jerusalem? "They said to me, 'The survivors who are left from the captivity …'" (verse 3). The Bible called them *survivors*. If you are a survivor, you are not thriving but you are just barely making it.

In the New Testament, Paul described Christians when he wrote in Romans: "We are more than conquerors through Him who loved us" (8:37). In the Greek, the word "conqueror" is *hupernekao*, which means "completely victorious." Paul wrote from prison: "We are more than conquerors." In that difficult situation, Paul was still thriving, while during the time of Nehemiah, the people in Jerusalem were merely surviving.

Which term best describes you? Are you just barely surviving, or are you more than a conqueror? The people in Jerusalem were just barely surviving because the city wall was broken and there were holes in it. Because of these breaches, the city was vulnerable. Terrorists could more easily mount an attack because the city was not secure.

In the old times, the ancient cities had walls around them. They would build up the walls and then they would put gates, which were portals to let people in and out. When you visualize the city gate, don't think of a little wooden gate on hinges flopping back and forth. The city gate of Jerusalem was a structure made of stone. It had at least two openings, which were often at right angles to each other. The city gate was the place of all the town action. If you walked into a city gate, you would see walls that enclosed a room that contained benches. The elders and the judges would sit on these benches. At the gate, you could exchange information, settle disputes, and have your case adjudicated.

If you were an enemy, you couldn't go directly into the city, but you would be taken through a portal and then you'd have to slow down and turn left or right because the openings were at right angles to each other. At each opening, a huge wooden door was covered with metal, so that it could not be easily burned or penetrated. If you were an army trying to attack the city, you could be trapped in that enclosure, called the gate. When you were trapped in the gate, people would shoot at you with arrows from above, or even pour hot oil on the attacking army. Gatekeepers and watchmen were important because they kept the city safe from intruders.

Here's the critical question for you: As a gatekeeper to your own soul and for your family's well-being, what are you letting in the gates? Of course, I'm using the same sort of metaphor the Apostle Paul used in 1 Corinthians 6:19, when he said, "Your body is the temple of the Holy Spirit." What's getting in your "eye gate" or your "ear gate" that shouldn't get in?

The ancients described seeing and hearing as the "eye gate" and the "ear gate." Through our daily use of the spiritual disciplines, we build up the walls of our lives. In the morning, when we read the Bible for our quiet time and we pray, we then obey what we read as principles that govern our lives during the day. This time in the Scriptures builds up the walls of our lives. Yet we have to guard the gates, or what we see and what we hear.

Think about a typical list of what you see on television, movies, the Internet, emails, newspapers, magazines, gossip. Each of those facets gets into you and affects your soul as they go through those gates of your eyes and ears. What good does it do to build up the walls if the gates are letting everything in? You may go through the various spiritual disciplines, such as reading or praying, but your gates are still unprotected.

One author gave this helpful description: "Picture your soul like a bowl of clear water." God intends your soul to be clean and clear. Every bad thought or image that you allow to enter through the eye gate or the ear gate is like a drop of food coloring. When a bad thought comes in or you see something or you hear something evil, one drop in the bowl. Then when you have another negative sight or sound, you get another drop of food coloring. By the end of the day, if those gates are freely letting anything in, you'll have a very murky bowl of water.

Solomon made this colorful description of the process in Proverbs 25:28: "Whoever has no rule over his own spirit [you could translate that his own soul] is like a city broken down, without walls" (words in brackets added). Doesn't that fit perfectly? The person without self-control is left open to ruin and is a victim of what he sees and what he hears. The first step is that you need to ask the right questions, such as "What is going on here?" You want to know the condition of your gates.

After asking the right questions, it should lead you to have the right reactions to what you learned. Notice Nehemiah's reaction in Nehemiah 1:3-4: "And they he said to me, 'The survivors who are left from the captivity in the province are there in great distress and reproach. The wall of Jerusalem is also broken down, and its gates are burned with fire.' So it was, when I heard these words, that I sat down and wept, and mourned for many days; I was fasting and praying before the God of heaven." What a strong reaction from a political figure in a Persian court! Nehemiah didn't hear the news and say, "Huh. Wow. Okay, whatever." He had a reaction to the information, which led him to craft a course of action.

Imagine you had two roommates and they both rented an apartment or a house together. One is Mr. Clean, or a neat freak, and one is Mr. Slob. The slob throws stuff anywhere he wants, piles up the dishes, washes them once a month, leaves his clothes everywhere, and when he comes home, he says, "What!?! This is organized!"

The actions of Mr. Slob are difficult for Mr. Clean to handle. After some time goes by, the house gets dirtier, the paint starts peeling from the walls, and little holes develop in the ceiling. For Mr. Slob, it is no big deal; he just puts bowls underneath to collect the water. When it's time to repair the house, which one is going to do it? It will not be Mr. Slob, but Mr. Clean, because he sees the problem and is moved to action. From his strong reaction, he'll be repairing their living space. Unless we see the problem and respond appropriately, we're never going to look for a remedy.

Do you remember how Jesus reacted when He saw the multitude coming to Him? The Scripture says, "He was moved with compassion" (Matthew 9:36). You never saw Jesus see a crowd and sigh, "I hate crowds. What do they want now? I just can't handle this." It never happened; instead Jesus was moved with compassion. He looked at the people as sheep without a shepherd.

What alarms you? What moves you? Whatever alarms or moves you will determine your course of action. I'm going to give you some statistics and ask if you're alarmed over some examples of soul thieves. Approximately forty million people in the United States are sexually involved with the Internet. It's hard to even put our heads around that number. Sex is the number-one topic that is searched for on the Internet. That position is not tenth or second or third; it's number one. Twenty-five percent of search engine requests, a fourth of everything searched for on the Internet, are pornographic. According to the Data Monitor Corporation, over one-half of all spending on the Internet is sex-related. At least twenty thousand American adults visit Internet sex sites for at least eleven hours each week.[3]

Are you alarmed yet? Listen to this: For every ten men in church, five are struggling with pornography. That's *half* of the men. Now before you women think, *Well, that's just a guy thing*, Mark O'Keefe of the *Charlotte Observer* wrote in an article: "Thirty-four percent of churchgoing women say they have intentionally visited porn websites online." That's staggering. And what's worse, according to the Barna Research Group, 38 percent of Americans find nothing morally wrong with these actions.

Dr. Victor Klein, of the University of Utah, writes: "Studies show that pornography is progressive and addictive for many. It can lead to the user acting out his fantasy, often on children." It's easy to see why, because children are weak, vulnerable, and trusting. Where do your children fall with this issue? It would seem the walls are broken down and the gates are burned with fire. According to the Internet Filter

Review, the largest consumer of Internet pornography is the age group from twelve to seventeen, because when kids are online, they're vulnerable and some people victimize them. One in seventeen children between the ages of ten and seventeen are threatened or harassed over the Internet. One in five children has been propositioned for cybersex on the Internet.[4]

You may ask, "Where does this happen?" It happens *in your home*, because 70 percent of sexual advances over the Internet occur while kids are on their home computers. Eighty-nine percent of those sexual solicitations were made in chat rooms. Parents, do you know what your children are chatting about online? Do you know some of the code language? For example, if you come across the letters *POS*, would you even know that means "Parent Over Shoulder"? For example, if you walked into the room and said, "Hey, what are you doing?" on the screen, you might read, "Let's move this conversation to a different thing now; I've got a POS, or parent over my shoulder." The teens have developed this code language for how to handle you in their lives.

All of this exposure skews our thinking, corrupts our hearts, and cuts our souls. For men, it changes the way they look at women, act toward women, and what they think is beautiful in a woman. It changes the way a husband looks at his wife, it changes women's attitude toward men, and it changes children. In the process of learning what is morally right and wrong, everything becomes skewed. This information should lead to the right reaction; that's why I asked the question about the degree of alarm that we feel from these statistics. Are you having the deep kind of reaction like Nehemiah and acting to find an answer to fight Internet pornography?

Let's return to Nehemiah 1 to see the third reaction from Nehemiah. After asking the questions, getting the information, and having a reaction, Nehemiah had to determine a course of action. When he took the right action, he did two things: one was spiritual and one was practical. Nehemiah first reached up toward God, and then he reached out to fix the problem. Nehemiah 1:5-11 says:

And I said, "I pray, LORD God of heaven, O great and awesome God, You who keep Your covenant and mercy with those who love You and observe Your commandments, please let Your ear be attentive and Your eyes open, that You may hear the prayer of Your servant which I pray before You now, day and night, for the children of Israel Your servants, and confess the sins of the children of Israel which we have sinned against You. Both my father's house and I have sinned. We have acted very corruptly against You, and have not kept the commandments, the statutes, nor the ordinances which You commanded Your servant Moses. Remember, I pray, the word that You commanded Your servant Moses, saying, 'If you are unfaithful, I will scatter you among the nations; but if you return to Me, and keep My commandments and do them, though some of you were cast out to the farthest part of the heavens, yet I will gather them from there, and bring them to the place which I have chosen as a dwelling for My name.' Now these are Your servants and Your people, whom You have redeemed by Your great power, and by Your strong hand. O Lord, I pray, please let Your ear be attentive to the prayer of Your servant, and to the prayer of Your servants who desire to fear Your name; and let

Your servant [that is, himself] prosper this day, I pray, and grant him mercy in the sight of this man [that is, King Artaxerxes]." For I was the king's cupbearer. (Words in brackets added).

First Nehemiah prayed to God, and then he reached out. His prayer was recorded in a rather lengthy section of chapter 1. In fact, the Book of Nehemiah has 406 verses and 46 verses, or 11 percent, of the book is made up of prayer. It showed Nehemiah's priorities, and it revealed his reaction when confronted with a problem. His first action was to pray.

Notice Nehemiah's language in his prayer. He didn't say, "Lord, I'm praying for those people; they're so bad." Instead Nehemiah used "we" language: "Both my father's house and I ["we"] have sinned" (Verse 6; words in brackets added). Instead of finger-pointing, Nehemiah acknowledged that he was part of the problem, so he could then be part of the solution. If you are a parent, I encourage you to pray every single day for your own soul and also for the souls, minds, and hearts of your children. It would be good if you prayed aloud in their presence. And when you pray, use "we" language, not pronouns like *them*, *they*, and *those*. Use words like *us* and *we*, such as, "Lord, forgive us and help us." I advise you to humble yourself in your children's sight and humble yourself in the eyes of the Lord in their presence. Through your example, they will understand, *Oh, that's how I'm supposed to live.* Nehemiah led through his example to the people.

After his prayer, Nehemiah got practical. In chapter 2 he stood before the king in his position of authority as cupbearer. Look at Nehemiah 2:5-6: "I said to the king, 'If it pleases the king, and if your servant has found favor in your sight, I ask that you send me to Judah, to the city of my fathers' tombs, that I may rebuild it.' Then the king said to me (with the queen also sitting beside him), 'How long will your journey be? And when will you return?' So it pleased the king to send me; and I set him a time."

Follow the progression of the story. First, Nehemiah sat down to weep, then he knelt down to pray, and then Nehemiah stood up to work. He knew there was only so long he could agonize; after a while it becomes time to organize. So he cried out, "O God, this is horrible." He didn't live in Jerusalem, but Nehemiah still did something about the situation. The king's cupbearer acted decisively and responsibly and said, "Send me. I want to rebuild the walls that are broken down."

What do we do to guard against the soul thieves in light of the information that we've just heard about our world? I think we must act decisively in our own homes. There are certain television channels we should block. (Usually you can block them on your own remote or you can call the company and say, "Block these channels, I don't want to see them.") When you hear this solution, you may protest, "Yeah, but I'm paying for those channels!" Just block them. Or you could set a schedule: "We watch television at a certain time for certain programs, but after this hour at night we don't." You should draw those lines of restriction for yourself as well as your family.

Now let's look at one final text in Scripture, found in Matthew 5. This chapter contains the first part of the Sermon on the Mount, the words of Jesus Christ. That day, Jesus was focused on the men in his audience, although as we have seen from the statistics, this is not exclusively a male problem. Matthew 5:27 says: "You have heard that it was said to those of old, 'You shall not commit adultery.'" The men in His audience were stroking their beards, thinking,

Yep, that's right. "But I say to you that whoever looks at a woman to lust for her has already committed adultery with her in his heart" (verse 28).

Oh, knife to the heart! Every man in that audience was slain that day and was feeling guilty. Naturally they thought, *Now what do I do?* In anticipation, Jesus answered: "If your right eye causes you to sin, pluck it out and cast it from you; for it is more profitable for you that one of your members perish, than for your whole body to be cast into hell" (Matthew 5:29). How's that for the bottom line in a message? "And if your right hand causes you to sin, cut it off and cast it from you; for it is more profitable for you that one of your members perish than for your whole body to be cast into hell" (verse 30).

If we are shocked by the words of Jesus, that was the intended effect. Jesus was saying to deal radically with sin. Don't compromise; deal radically with it, avoid it at all costs, and do whatever is necessary to avoid it. Martin Luther said: "You can't stop birds from flying over your head, but you can stop them from building a nest in your hair." Don't be the devil's dartboard; instead, flee temptation. What does that mean? It means flee, run, walk away, change channels, turn it off, get out, call someone, and flee.

One night at about midnight a doctor called his pastor. This doctor had just been called to the hospital for an emergency situation. A young woman was brought in who had been beaten mercilessly beyond recognition; in fact, many of the bones in her body were broken. Her boyfriend had beat her up. As they brought this woman from the emergency room to the operating suite, they knew that the only hope for saving her life was direct contact with the heart, or a cardiac massage. So they opened her up and began to massage the heart, but she didn't make it through the operation. After she died, the hospital staff was attempting to learn the identity of this young lady, so they went through her purse. They discovered used hypodermic needles. She was a drug user who was living with her boyfriend, also a drug user. In addition, they learned the young woman was HIV-positive, and that's when the doctor became alarmed. Speaking with his pastor, the doctor said, "As we were doing the operation, I accidentally cut my finger through the glove into the skin on one of the broken ribs around the heart."

The pastor said, "Is that really a huge problem?" He was a pastor, not a doctor.

The doctor said, "Pastor, even a paper-thin cut, when you are in direct contact with that polluted bloodstream, is enough to infect you with AIDS."

How many paper-thin cuts to your soul do you allow? What are you letting through your "eye gate" or your "ear gate"? The clear water of the soul can become infected and grow murky. Like Nehemiah, you can say to the Lord today, "I want to rebuild my walls and those gates that are broken down. I'm going to figure out ways to have gatekeepers and wall builders because of the attacks on my soul and my family's soul. I will be careful what I let into my heart."

IS THE CHURCH SECURE?

How many Christians does it take to change a lightbulb? It's a long-standing joke, and you've probably heard many variations of it. The answer is, it depends. If they are Presbyterians, none, because the lights will go on and off at predestined times. If they are Catholics, none, because they use candles. If they are Baptists, it takes at least fifteen: one to change the lightbulb and three committees to approve the change and then decide who brings the potato salad. If they are Episcopalians, it will take three to change the lightbulb and one to call the electrician, one to mix the drinks, and one to talk about how much better the old one was. If they are charismatics, then it will take only one to change the lightbulb because their hands are already in the air. If they are Pentecostals, then it takes ten: one to change the bulb and nine to pray against the spirit of darkness. Unitarians simply say, "We choose not to make a statement either in favor of or against the need for a lightbulb. If, however, in your own journey you find that lightbulbs work for you, then that is fine. You are invited to write a poem or compose a modern dance about your lightbulb for next Sunday's service, in which we will explore a number of perditions including incandescent, fluorescent, three-way, long-life, and tinted, all of which are equally valid paths to luminescence." If they are Methodists, then it takes an undetermined number depending on whether your light is bright, dull, or completely out. They also say, "A churchwide Methodist lighting service is planned for next Sunday, so bring the bulb of your choice and a covered dish." If they are Nazarenes, then it takes six: one woman to replace the bulb while five men review the church lighting policy. If they are Lutherans, then it takes no one because Lutherans don't believe in change. But if they are Amish, then they are asking, "What's a lightbulb?"

Okay, now that I've offended every tradition possible, I should share my point to this illustration. While we're busy talking about insignificant things like changing lightbulbs, some people in the world would like to extinguish our light altogether.

In this chapter, I want to discuss an idea most of us don't even like to even entertain, which is the concept of persecution. As we follow Jesus Christ, none of us signed up for persecution, yet the Bible says, "All who desire to live godly in Christ Jesus will suffer persecution" (2 Timothy 3:12). Some of you may be thinking, *This has nothing at all to do with my life; I've never been persecuted.* That lack of persecution is not necessarily a good sign! You might be experiencing the peace of having no persecution like the peace of the draft-dodger who, during the Vietnam War, went up to Canada thinking, *Life rocks here, man. I've got no problems.* You're not in the battle. But if you ever get in the battle, by your lifestyle and by preaching the gospel, you *will* suffer persecution.

I understand that right now, in the West, persecution as such is virtually unheard of, but I want to tell you about how things are changing. Opposition to the gospel has been around since the time of Jesus Christ and is prevalent in many places of the world. Last year in Lebanon, I had the privilege of speaking at a pastor's conference where pastors attended from several Middle Eastern countries: Lebanon, Syria, Iraq, Jordan, Egypt, and a few from Sudan. This leadership conference was attended by pastors and their spouses, and they were talking about the hostile environments they faced, how people have threatened them and their families. Yet these believers had a quality that I longed for those of us in the West to possess. These men and women had an unspeakable joy as they counted it worthy to suffer for Christ.

How safe is the Church? That's a question that has been raised recently. One Sunday morning in Colorado, a man walked into a YWAM base and blew two people away. Then he went to a church in Colorado Springs, shot five people—two died in church. Days earlier, this man had sent hateful emails and blogged about how he hated these groups, threatening that some would lose their lives.

Do you believe the Church is secure? I can give you a resounding answer, "Yes! From a heavenly perspective, it is absolutely secure." Jesus said: "I will build My church, and the gates of Hades shall not prevail against it" (Matthew 16:18). You're on a winning team, and I've read the end of the book—we win! Yet what happens before we finally win? What is the future of the Church worldwide, and especially in America? And if persecution is coming, how do we prepare for it?

I want to alert you to three basic movements in our Bible passage. Jesus told His disciples what to expect in their future, and it was something they didn't bargain on hearing.

And then He told them why they were going to experience it. Finally, Jesus told them what to do, or how to respond to persecution.

I want to begin in Luke 21 and look at a few verses. The theme of this chapter is the Second Coming of Jesus Christ. Our primary verse is Luke 21:27, in which Jesus promised He would come back in power and glory. But before verse 27, Jesus told us what would happen in the world and in our lives before He returns. For instance, in Luke 21:8, Jesus told His disciples to expect religious deception: "Take heed that you not be deceived. For many will come in My name, saying, 'I am He,' and, 'The time has drawn near.' Therefore do not go after them."

The world can expect false religious expressions, which has always been the case outside the Church with various religious groups and cults; even inside the Church, these groups have proliferated and will continue to proliferate until the end. Then, Luke 21:9-10 tell us to expect international conflict: "When you hear of wars and commotions, do not be terrified, for these things must come to pass first, but the end will not come immediately." Then He said to them: "Nation will rise against nation, and kingdom against kingdom."

These events in our world don't surprise us when they happen because Jesus said they would happen before He comes again.

Third, Jesus told us about forthcoming natural disasters. Luke 21:11 said: "There will be great earthquakes in various places, and famines and pestilence; there will be fearful sights and great signs from heaven." As Jesus was going through this list with His disciples, I have a hunch that they didn't expect this information. As Jews at the time, these disciples had a certain fixed theology. They believed Jesus was the Messiah and they believed that once the Messiah arrived, then He was there for good. He was not going to leave and return at a later time. In fact, they expected the Messiah to conquer Rome, destroy the enemies of the Jews, and then set himself up as king over Israel. These disciples expected to rule and reign with Jesus in positions of power, authority, and influence.

As the disciples listened to Jesus in Luke 21, suddenly it sounded like it would be a long time before He returned to rule and to reign. He talked first about religious deception and then wars and conflicts, and finally natural disasters. Then in the middle of their growing concern, it suddenly became worse, because in Luke 21:12, the real shocker arrived: "But before all these things, they will lay their hands on you and persecute you, delivering you up to the synagogues and prisons. You will be brought before kings and rulers for My name's sake."

These words are the opposite from their expectations, and it was hard for them to understand. In fact, they didn't understand at all, because in the very next chapter, they argued about who would be the greatest in the kingdom and who would sit at His right hand and left hand in glory. The disciples bypassed everything Jesus said about persecution and wars. They didn't even get it after Jesus died and then rose from the dead. In Acts 1, their first question was, "Will you at this time restore the kingdom to Israel?"

Let's return to Luke 21:12 and study it in detail. First, Jesus said you can expect the religious establishment to hate you. Or, as He said: "[They will deliver] you up to the synagogues and prisons." At that time in history, the synagogue was also the local court, where civil and criminal cases were heard and then adjudicated by twenty-three judges. The disciples expected the synagogue, and the entire nation of Israel, to receive Jesus as their Messiah. This idea that Israel would completely and totally reject Jesus as the Messiah was unexpected.

Second, the secular world was going to hate believers. Or as Jesus said: "You will be brought before kings and rulers." At that time the Jews had no king. They were under a foreign Gentile power, and so this statement was not what the disciples expected. These followers of Jesus expected Him to conquer the Romans, and instead the Romans crucified Jesus.

Next let's skip down to Luke 21:16, where the situation grows even worse. Jesus said: "You will be betrayed even by parents and brothers, relatives and friends; and they will put some of you to death." For the disciples, this was almost more than they could handle: Israel was going to reject Jesus. He wasn't going to take over the world, but the world was going to crucify Him. It was beyond their understanding that Jesus would die and leave them before He ever ruled the world. And then, in Luke 21:16, Jesus said the whole world was going to gang up on Christians.

While these words were the complete antithesis of their beliefs, it is what happened. If you read through the Book of Acts, you see that as soon as the gospel was preached in Jerusalem, the synagogues rose up against the believers. Wherever the gospel was taken in Jewish or Gentile territory, the disciples were arrested, betrayed, and even killed.

If you want to follow Church history, I recommend you read *Foxe's Book of Martyrs*, which outlines stories of brothers and sisters who have suffered great persecution because they believed in Jesus Christ. For instance, the Romans flung members of the early Church to the lions, while other believers were burned at the stake. Nero tied them up to poles, poured hot pitch on them while they were still alive, and then set the pitch aflame so that at night the Christians became living torches in his gardens. On other occasions, because Nero knew Christians called Jesus the "Good Shepherd," he thought, *Let's see if your Shepherd will protect you*. He took lambskins, wrapped Christians in these carcasses, and then threw them to the wild dogs, lions, and wolves in the arenas while saying, "Let's see if your Shepherd will protect you." The wild animals ate the Christians alive. Other stories tell about molten lead being poured on them while they were alive. Other believers had their eyes gouged out or parts of their bodies cut off and then roasted before their eyes. These events were unexpected to the disciples of Jesus, certainly not what they wanted to hear.

When you became a Christian, what did you expect would happen? This week I was thinking about how the decision is usally framed for nonbelievers today. The witnesses would say something like, "Look, we want you to give your life to Jesus Christ and surrender totally to Him. If you take this step, you're going to be forgiven of all of your sins and discover a peace in your life that you've never experienced before, plus you're going to be in Heaven for the rest of eternity." Believers need to add: "But you should also understand that from here on out, people are going to hate you, turn against you, and even your own family is going to shun you."

How many people would say, "Where do I sign up?" When you became a believer, maybe you thought, *I'm going to have health and prosperity. I'm going to escape all of my problems.* At least that's what the televangelists are always saying on TV. Jesus told the disciples what they could expect before His coming, and it looks very grim. Persecution has always been around.

Most of us tend to think of persecution as something that happened a long time ago. But during the last year, it has been estimated that 160,000 Christians were killed for their faith in Christ. If you follow the reports, in Sudan, Christians have been sold into slavery. In Indonesia, Muslim radicals have burned the villages of Christians. During the twentieth century, more Christians were martyred than in any other century in history. This means that in this last century more Christians were killed than in the first century or in the second or third or fourth century! One report says 100 million Christians have been martyred.[1]

If you took the whole Church worldwide, it is estimated that one in every two hundred Christians can expect to be martyred in his or her lifetime. You maybe be thinking, *I didn't understand this was part of the package.* Now, most of this persecution happens outside of the United States and we don't usually see this inside our borders. But you need to be aware that persecution may be coming, and Jesus wanted us to be aware of it. In fact, we're seeing more vocal, aggressive, hostile language and movement toward believers, even in this country. At first the United States got rid of prayer in schools, then they debated about the public display of the Ten Commandments, and finally they attempted to take the words "under God" out of the Pledge of Allegiance. The notorious organization, the ACLU, has spearheaded most of these movements. This organization has a stated agenda to "ensure the first amendment, the separation of Church and state," yet they twist the concept in order to remove any trace of religion from America, especially Christianity.

Here's a sampling: In California, the ACLU sued the National Park Service because they wanted a cross removed from a World War I veterans' memorial. They said, "There's a cross on it; we've got to get rid of it. You're violating the separation of Church and state." So they sued the State of California.

Next, the ACLU went after the city of Los Angeles because their seal displayed a cross, among many other spiritual icons. They said, "You've got to get rid of that." All of this, despite California history, which includes men like Father Euniporasera, who started twenty-one missions, and a huge religious background. Then the ACLU went after the city of Redlands, California, because their seal of the city also included a cross. The ACLU said, "Under clearly established law, this seal is unconstitutional." While such a claim is bogus, the ACLU is so vigorous, aggressive, and intimidating that most people fold when they are confronted.

In *The Criminalization of Christianity*, Janet Folger writes: "There is a war going on for the future of our country. Most people know that, but what they may not know is that if Christians lose, the result won't just be public policy with which we disagree, it will be a prison sentence for those who disagree."

Next she explains, "I was prepared to make a prediction in this book that many of you wouldn't have believed. I had written it down as an unbelievable, outrageous possibility. I was going to say that if we remain silent in this battle, pastors will go to jail for speaking about homosexuality in their own pulpits in their own churches. But before I could even finish this first chapter, it already happened." Then she cites the case: "A Swedish court has sentenced a pastor belonging to the Pentecostal movement in Sweden—Aiche Greene; he's in his seventies—a month in prison under a law against incitement after he was found guilty of having offended homosexuals in a sermon. Soren Anderson, the president of the Swedish Federation for Lesbian, Gay, Bisexual, and Trans-Gender Rights, said in a hearing that religious freedom could never be used as a reason to offend people. Therefore he told the journalist, 'I cannot regard the sentence as an act of interference with the freedom of religion.' It happened."

In Elmira, New York, the police arrested seven Christians for praying in a public park where a gay festival was about to get underway. These believers in Jesus didn't say anything, protest, or even hold up a sign. All they did was get down on their knees and begin to pray, and then they were arrested. In Philadelphia, Pennsylvania, two women in their seventies, both of them grandmothers, plus nine other people, were arrested for sharing their faith on a public sidewalk. Because of a Pennsylvania ruling against hate crimes, these Christians face a possible sentence of forty-seven years in prison because they shared their faith in Christ.

Some of you might be thinking, *Skip, how is any of this appealing to me? How is any of what you just said ever going to attract people to Christianity?*

I'll tell you this, persecution beats the alternative. I would much rather go through all of the temporary rejection from this world than the eternal rejection of God. Jesus described eternity in hell as a place with wailing, gnashing of teeth, and everlasting fire. In light of that perspective, the temporary situation in our world begins to fade in importance. Jesus predicted this unexpected future for His disciples.

Next let's look at the unavoidable reason why this will happen. At the end of Luke 21:12, notice: "You will be brought before kings and rulers for My name's sake." And Luke 21:17 says: "You will be hated by all for My name's sake."

Jesus said, "They're going to persecute you because they hate me." It's not because Christians are ornery or unkind or unlovely (though sometimes they can be). Persecution will happen because Christians represent Jesus and the gospel. For a minute, think about the gospel message: It is not inclusive; in fact, it is very exclusive.

The good news about Jesus *can* include everyone. Jesus died for the sins of the whole world. Any person in any country, of any language, of any age, at any time, can come to Jesus Christ and have their sins forgiven. But the gospel message says that only those who receive Christ as Lord and Savior will enter Heaven. All those who reject Him will be eternally lost. That's not an appealing message, and in fact, it angers many people who hate the message of the gospel. No wonder when Peter was preaching, Acts 2 says: "Now when they heard this [that is the message about Christ], they were cut to the heart" (Verse 37; words in brackets added). The Good News about Jesus was not what they wanted to hear.

This week I received an email from someone who claims to be a believer. I don't know this person, but he said, "I don't understand why every religion thinks they have the special attention of God. It appears to me that Christians are no better than Muslims." This narrow gospel is a tough message. Listen, if there were 485 ways to God, then I'd preach all 485 of them, but they don't exist.

If I take a plain, simple reading of Scripture, there is only one way to Heaven, and that angers people. Jesus said, "Your persecution is on account of me. It's for my name's sake." That's the unavoidable fact, and here's the principle: Great persecution is simply a result of the Great Commission. If you go into the entire world and preach the gospel, you're going to get persecuted. All those who live godly lives in Christ Jesus will suffer persecution. Jesus said in John 15:25: "If the world hates you, you know that it hated Me before it hated you.... This happened that the word might be fulfilled which is written in their law, 'They hated Me without a cause.'"

Have you ever had someone just hate you for no reason. "Why don't you like me?"

"I don't know. I just hate you."

"Well, why?"

"I just do."

If that sounds unfair, Jesus had first dibs on it when He told us, "They hated me without a cause. If they hate you, it's because they hate me."

The other night, I was listening to a short MP3 broadcast of Madelyn Murray O'Hare. If you remember, she was the vocal forerunner of the atheistic movement in America. Over the years, I followed her work until her death in 1995. I was listening to her debate with Walter Martin. Throughout the recording, her language was especially demeaning, vitriolic, and hostile toward Christians. She said, "Christianity is intolerant, anti-democratic anti-sexual and anti-life. It is anti-woman, and I cannot stand that. It is anti-everything that is good and human and decent and kind and love-filled and understanding. I used to have an intellectual hatred for Christianity. I think that is broadening now. I'm enjoying hating the whole thing." The persecution of Christianity is based on the unavoidable factor of "My name's sake."

How are we to meet persecution? What do we do? It takes unswerving followers to successfully overcome persecution. I know, you received Jesus Christ and it was wonderful, and you thought, *Life rocks; this is great.* Then all of a sudden, life got hard. People began to laugh at you, and your family rejected you. You lost a job or a relationship because of your relationship with Jesus, and it became very difficult.

Where do you find the strength to handle it? *First, you believe in His promise.* Look at Luke 21:18: "But not a hair of your head shall be lost." What does that mean? Jesus just said: "They're going to hate you and kill you" (see verse 17).

Luke 21:18 does not mean Christians are somehow exempt from all this suffering. That interpretation would not make sense because it would contradict what Jesus just said. But look at Matthew 10:28-30. Jesus said:

> "Do not fear those who kill the body but cannot kill the soul. But rather fear Him who is able to destroy both soul and body in hell. Are not two sparrows sold for a copper coin? And not one of them falls to the ground apart from your Father's will. But the very hairs of your head are all numbered."

Jesus was simply saying, "I and my Father take personal care and concern whenever one of our children is being persecuted and mistreated." Even sparrows don't fall to the ground without God's awareness and care, so these things (persecution) aren't going to happen without your Father's knowledge. He takes special interest and concern. Jesus gave us this promise because when the world treats us poorly, we're apt to think, *Where's God? He doesn't care. Look what's happening to me.*

But Jesus would say, "Not a hair of your head shall be lost." Whatever you lose on this Earth—for example, if you lose a boyfriend because of your relationship with Christ; if you lose a job; even if you get killed—ultimately you will be ushered into Heaven. When you are there, I can guarantee you're never going to look back at what you lost. The rewards are going to be so great. Jesus said: "Rejoice and be exceedingly glad [when you are persecuted], for great is your reward in heaven" (Matthew 5:12). In faith, you believe His promise.

Second, you persevere. Luke 21:19 says: "By your patience possess your souls." Isn't that sort of an enigma? In the New English Bible, this passage translates: "By standing firm you will win true life for yourselves." This same idea is expressed elsewhere when Jesus said, "He who endures to the end will be saved" (Matthew 24:13; see also Mark 13:13).

Here's the problem: Life is good, and then life gets bad. When life gets bad, we want to say, "I quit. I didn't sign up for this." If you would just hold on and persevere and keep going, you're eventually going to be even more blessed. The problem is, we often want to quit. Jesus encourages us: "Don't quit. Keep persevering; keep going through it; there's an even bigger blessing at the end."

For a moment, let's recall those Lebanese, Syrian, Iraqi, and Jordanian pastors whom I saw, and their unspeakable joy. Don't quit. In fact, maybe it would be better to not pray for a lighter load, but pray for a stronger backs.

We can be assured the assaults are going to come. When assaults come, trust the Lord and stay the course. As I wrap this chapter, let me give two quick ways to stay the course from Matthew 5.

Your first way to stay the course is to shine your light. The world wants to put out your light. Don't argue about lightbulbs. Instead, turn on the light and share Christ with other people. Tell them the truth and don't back down. The Apostle Peter said we should always be ready to give a reason, an answer, or a defense for the hope that lives in us (see 1 Peter 3:15). But when you have such an answer of hope, Peter said to provide that answer with meekness and reverence. Don't beat people over the head with the gospel and tell them, "You wretched, foul sinner, you're going to hell. That's the good news." Instead, as you shine the light, use a soft answer that turns away wrath.

The second way to stay the course is to spread your salt. As Christians, we're called to be salt and light. Thankfully we live in America, not the ancient Roman Empire. Because we don't have a Caesar ruling over us, we have a part in the process, choices we can make. We can vote, get involved in setting policy, and make what we believe count. You can make a difference. If you don't spread your salt, then every year, you'll complain how bad it is—yet you never did anything at all to change it. We live in a country where we can take an active role. Yet I want to warn you about that role. Christians tend to think that for the gospel to flourish in America, we have to have righteous politics and righteous government. That is not true. In fact, if you look at history, the gospel flourished when Christians were the most persecuted and the most hated. Take the ancient Roman Empire and the current cultural revolution in China. Today a hundred million Christians were brought into the kingdom out of great persecution. Get involved, spread the salt, shine the light, and trust the Lord. Is the Church secure? Absolutely yes, and the gates of hell will not prevail against it.

When I was a kid in school, I wasn't great at sports. I did them because I had to do them, but I wasn't really great at any of them. When it was time to pick teams, I hated it, because I knew I wouldn't get picked first, or second, or even third. I'd be the kid hanging around thinking, *I hope someone eventually picks me.* Yet I knew that if the team captains were either Duane Moore or David McCackley, I wanted to be on either of their teams. Those would be winning teams, because those guys knew how to strategize and they were great athletes. I was hoping I would get picked to be on one of those teams. Today, you can know you are on the winning team. Jesus has picked you to be on His team.

Back in the 1870s, there was an old hymn that has been sung throughout the years since then: "Onward Christian soldiers, marching as to war, with the cross of Jesus going on before."[2] The concept for this hymn was based on 2 Timothy, which says: "Endure hardness as a good soldier of Jesus Christ" (2 Timothy 2:3, KJV). Let's march onward.

Let's not follow the words of some author who changed the words of that hymn to read, "Backward Christian soldiers, fleeing from the fight, with the cross of Jesus nearly out of sight. Christ our rightful master, stands against the foe, onward into battle, we seem afraid to go."[3] Let's not shrink from this battle. Let's march into the future together preaching the gospel!

The question isn't, how many Christians does it take to change a lightbulb? The real question is this: How many Christians does it take to shine the light? The answer is, just one. Jesus needs just one Christian who will be bold enough at work, at school, and in the neighborhood. Stand up, turn on the light, and share Jesus.

You may think, *People won't like me.* They didn't like Jesus. Or you may think, *People will be mean to me.* They were mean to Jesus. But remember, great will be your reward in Heaven.

Chapter 8

CASUALTIES ON THE BATTLEFIELD OF FAITH

About 1,600 years ago, during the fourth century, the Church was unsettled. The Christians were up-in-arms, all the way from Constantinople, in modern-day Turkey, down to Alexandria, Egypt. Why? They were wrestling with some of the key foundational issues about life and their belief system, such as: Who is God? What about Jesus? Is there a Trinity?

A man named Arius of Alexandria, Egypt, began denying Jesus was God, denying the Trinity, and casting aspersions on the character and work of Christ.[1] To respond, three hundred leaders convened in A.D. 325 in a little town called Nicaea, which is in modern-day Turkey. They formulated a statement of their beliefs, now called the Nicene Creed. They said, "We believe in one God, the Father, the Almighty, the Maker of heaven and earth, of all that is, seen and unseen. We believe in one Lord Jesus Christ, the only Son of God, eternally begotten of the Father, God from God, light from light, true God from true God, begotten and not made, of one substance with the Father. We believe in the Holy Spirit."[2] The creed continues but details absolutes that are unshakeable, nonnegotiable, and the core of the faith. They knew these facts to be true.

Things have changed, and people today aren't so certain what they believe. Even inside the Church, they're not so sure. Mark Twain said, "A lie can travel halfway around the world while truth is still tying its shoes."[3] It's amazing what gets printed as truth. Here are a few extreme examples from the tabloid newspapers in the grocery store: "Alien mummy goes on a rampage."[4] "Cow mattresses help cows produce more milk." "Mom-to-be on a diet of only chicken lays a huge egg." "World War II bomber found on the moon." "Woman gives birth to two-year-old baby; child walks and talks in three days." Can you believe these stories were printed and people bought it?

The Apostle Paul wrote part of 2 Timothy to his young protégé, who was left in the city of Ephesus. It is about apostasy, in which people fall away or depart from the truth. When this book was written, it had only been thirty years since Jesus was on the Earth and the Gospel first penetrated the ancient world. Yet now, people were dropping like flies and becoming casualties on the battlefield of truth. On the one hand, it isn't surprising because that's how it's been since the beginning, when God first revealed himself to man. In the Garden, Satan said to Eve, "Has God said ...?" and then challenged the revelation of God. In Luke 18:8, even Jesus asked the penetrating question: "When the Son of Man comes [or returns], will He really find faith on the earth?" (Words in brackets added). Isn't that a provocative question?

In the last chapter, we learned how there is an attack on the historic Christian faith from the outside. Now I want to look at a trend that is even more disturbing—an attack from inside the realm of the Church. I'm going to mention some movements and names with which you may or may not be familiar. One movement has been around and ongoing since the 1990s under an umbrella called the Emerging Church movement. To a large part, this movement denies that you can know anything in an absolute way. This movement is repackaged liberalism and existentialism. In some places this movement is called Christian evangelicalism, and many people don't know the difference.

Once Abraham Lincoln had a heated argument and finally asked the disputer, "How many legs does a cow have?"

The man said, "Four, of course."

"Good," Lincoln said. "Now suppose you call the tail of the cow a leg. Now how many legs does the cow have?"

The disputer said, "Five."

Lincoln said, "That's where you're wrong. It doesn't matter how many times you call a tail a leg, a cow still only has four legs."[5] The same truth applies to these untrue movements. Calling something truth doesn't make it true.

I want to draw your attention to the first four verses of 2 Timothy 4, in which Paul wrote to Timothy:

> I charge you [and the word is, I *solemnly* charge you] therefore before God and the Lord Jesus Christ, who will judge the living and the dead at His appearing and His kingdom. Preach the word! Be ready in season and out of season. Convince, rebuke, exhort, with all longsuffering and teaching. For the time will come when they will not endure sound doctrine, but according to their own desires, because they have itching ears, they will heap up for themselves teachers; and they will turn their ears away from the

truth, and be turned again or turned aside to fables. But you be watchful in all things, endure afflictions, do the work of an evangelist, fulfill your ministry." (Words in brackets added.)

Timothy was leading the church in Ephesus, where Paul had left him to pastor the believers. Yet Ephesus had an undercurrent of apostasy. And you'll notice even in the first verse, the words, "I charge you therefore before God" (2 Timothy 4:1). I've mentioned before this rule of thumb for studying the Scriptures: Whenever there's a "therefore," you need to find out "what it's there for." Paul wasn't introducing a new thought, but he was building off the thoughts that were previously discussed.

Let's turn back a few pages to 2 Timothy 1 to follow Paul's line of thinking. In 2 Timothy 1:13-15, Paul wrote:

Hold fast the pattern of sound words which you have heard from me, in faith and love which are in Christ Jesus. That good thing which was committed to you, keep by the Holy Spirit who dwells in us. This you know, that all those in Asia have turned away from me, among whom are Phygellus and Hermogenes.

Because Paul used specific names, these people are unfortunately forever inscribed in the Scriptures in a negative light.

Now let's look at 2 Timothy 2:15: "Be diligent to present yourself approved to God, a worker who does not need to be ashamed, rightly dividing the word of truth." I want you to take that little phrase, "word of truth," and keep it in the front of your brain, because you're going to need it in just a minute. Second Timothy 2:16-18 says:

But shun profane and idle babblings, for they will increase to more ungodliness. And their message will spread like cancer. Hymenaeus and Philetus are of this sort [again, he names two other men], who have strayed concerning the truth, saying that the resurrection has already past; and they overturn the faith of some." (Words in brackets added.)

Second Timothy 3:1-4 says:

But know this, that in the last days perilous times will come. For men will be lovers of themselves, lovers of money, boasters, proud, blasphemers, disobedient to parents, unthankful, unholy, unloving, unforgiving, slanderers, without self-control, brutal, despisers of good, traitors, headstrong, haughty, lovers of pleasure rather than lovers of God.

While this last verse was a pretty bad description, on top of all that, the same group in 2 Timothy 3:5-7 was:

... having a form of godliness but denying its power. And from such people turn away! For of this sort are those who creep into households and make captives of gullible women loaded down with sins, led away by various lusts, always learning and never able to come to the knowledge of the truth.

Only thirty years after Jesus walked the Earth, the truth was perverted. That didn't take long! These warnings were not just given in Timothy; there are many other warnings given in the letters of Paul, and even in some of the words of Jesus. This undercurrent about falling away or departing from the truth is found throughout the New Testament. For example in 2 Thessalonians 2:3, Paul wrote about the Second Coming of Christ: "That Day will not come unless the falling away comes first." He was referring to the apostasy, or the departure from the truth. It says: "The Second Coming of Christ won't occur until the end times. There's going to be a huge departure from the truth."

Then 1 Timothy 1:19 says: "Concerning the faith [many] have suffered shipwreck." Then in 2 Peter 2, Peter wrote that there "will be false teachers among you, who will secretly bring in destructive heresies" (verse 1). The beloved Apostle John chimed in 1 John 2:19, saying: "They went out from us, but they were not of us; for if they had been of us, they would have continued with us." Finally, Jesus Christ spoke about apostasy in Revelation 2 and 3 in seven short letters to seven churches. He gave each of them a report card and said: "I know your works, I know this about you, I know that about you.... " (See 2:2, 9, 13, 19; 3:1, 8, 15.) In almost every letter, Jesus said, "Nevertheless I have this against you." Jesus tells the church in Ephesus: "You have left your first love" (2:4). Then to another church,[6] Jesus said they followed the doctrine of Balaam, while yet a different church listened to a woman called Jezebel. Each of these churches represents a departure from the truth.

The New Testament contains many warnings, and here's the reason why: The Church has always been right in the middle of the battle for truth. Follow my thinking: Because the Church has always been at the forefront in the battle for truth, Paul called this matter to their attention in 1 Timothy 3:15: "The church of the living God, the pillar and ground of all truth."

If the Church is the pillar and the ground of all truth, the theater for the spiritual battle will be the Church. That's why we're not surprised when liberalism enters the Church. Nor are we surprised when cults try to come into the Church or when attacks and splits happen to the Church, because the Church is ground zero. As the New Testament warns, each of us needs to be on our guard and discerning of what is taking place in the Church.

One name that has been around for many years is called the WCC, or the World Council of Churches. It's comprised of about 350 churches, organizations, and denominations. They claim 560 million adherents.[7] And doesn't the name sound good? It sounds as if they are all getting together and promoting unity through their council. Their headquarters is located in Geneva, Switzerland. Recently twenty-five theologians gathered in this consortium and said, "All religions and all religious traditions are ambiguous."[8] In other words, each religion is a combination of good and bad: "We need to move beyond a theology which confines salvation to the explicit personal commitment to Jesus Christ." These church leaders said, "We've got to move beyond Jesus." One of the WCC theologians is a Korean named Chung Hyun Kyung,[9] who said, "I have discovered that my bowel is a Shamanist bowel, my heart is a Buddhist heart, and my head is a Christian head."[10] I have no idea what he is saying, but he is certainly not a part of the true Church of Jesus Christ.

Let's return to the Emerging Church. In the 1990s when it began, I believe it was founded with a good idea. A group of people got together and said, "How do we have church in a postmodern age?" They wanted to upgrade the music, upgrade the style, and create an up-to-date church for the next generation." These changes are excellent when you're talking about style. But it becomes a different arena when you're talking about substance, doctrine, and truth. Under this umbrella of the Emerging Church, other streams started flowing in, creating an amorphous movement that is now a moving target, difficult to pin down and define. This situation isn't true of every church under the Emerging label, but by and large, they question the notion of absolute truth. As one leader said, "The concept of absolute truth is a rationalization of the worst sort." This means that when you talk about sin, we're unsure what that is; when you talk about salvation, we're unsure what that is, too. This can become very confusing.

This type of talk about the Church can be related to cars. For example, let's say you had a brand-new red Lexus loaded with the works, like side air bags, front air bags, iPod player, GPS, and an automatic emergency brake. As you drove your red Lexus, someone came up to you and said, "How do you know it's a Lexus? I think it sort of looks like an Oldsmobile."

Then another person comes to you and says, "How do you know it's red? Maybe it's blue and you just think its red."

A different person sees your Lexus and asks, "How do you know it really works? Did you really pay that much for it? Does it really have side air bags? Does the iPod work? Does it really have automatic emergency brakes?"

Finally someone asks you, "How do you even know it's a car?"

This is the approach of many people within the Emerging Church movement.

In 2 Timothy 4:1, Paul was talking about the prevalent condition because there is a coming evaluation. Everyone should be concerned about the coming of Christ that is on the horizon. Second Timothy 4:1 says: "I charge you therefore before God and the Lord Jesus Christ, who will judge the living and the dead at His appearing [the first stage, for His

Church] and His kingdom [the second stage]" (words in brackets added).

While there is a great deal of information in this verse, essentially Paul was saying, "Listen, young Timothy, because you're going to have to stand before God and give an account for your ministry, so preach the Word." Ultimately none of us are going to have to give an account before our mom or our dad or our son or our daughter or our pastor or a committee or a board or a denomination. Our ultimate accounting will be before God, and the big issue won't be whether you're hip enough, cool enough, postmodern enough, or edgy enough. The real issue is going to be whether you were faithful to the truth.

I don't know about you, but when I hear about the return of Jesus Christ, I get pretty excited. I don't know when Jesus is going to return, and I'm not going to make any predictions. But I get excited because historically and since the beginning, the return of Jesus Christ has been the culmination of our Christian hope. When Jesus returns, He's going to deal with us, judge the world, and make things right, which has always been the Christian hope. As we pray in the Lord's Prayer, "Thy kingdom come." We get excited about this event because many times the Bible points to it. In fact, 1,845 times there is a direct reference or an allusion to the Second Coming of Christ. For every single time Jesus' first coming is mentioned, there are about eight mentions of the Second Coming. Jesus spoke about His return twenty-one times and fifty times in the Bible we're told to be ready for it. This culmination of our hope has been the inspiration of songs throughout the ages. Even Julia Ward Howe's "Battle Hymn of the Republic" begins with the phrase, "Mine eyes have seen the glory of the coming of the Lord." And consider "Joy to the World" by Isaac Watts, which was not actually written about Christmas, although today we have conveniently used this song to celebrate that season.[11] The words are about the Second Coming of Jesus, including the first line of the song: "Joy to the world, the Lord is come. Let earth receive her king." Or think about the words to the hymn "How Great Thou Art." This phrase is about the return of Christ:"When Christ shall come, with shouts of acclamation, and take me home, what joy will fill my heart."

While much of the Bible points to the return of Jesus, many leaders in the Emerging Church movement would point you away from it. In fact, they would say that to talk about looking for Jesus Christ's return is a silly notion and alienating to most people.

One of the Emerging Church leaders, Rob Bell, said, "To preach about the return of Jesus Christ for the church and the following judgment is a horrible and toxic message." Oh, really? The Bible calls the return of Jesus Christ "the blessed hope," not a horrible, toxic message. Bell also said, "The whole system that says a few people because of what they said, did, or believe in are going to heaven and everyone else is going to hell, is a deeply flawed system and must die." With this sentence, Bell puts into question our salvation and eternal security in Heaven. As followers of Jesus Christ, we are to be spiritually alert. Here's the bottom line: Because of the truth of the Scriptures, we know too much to be cavalier, apathetic, or uncertain. Instead, we have a responsibility to be on the alert in these matters. W. G. Burns once said, "A Christian is not likely to fall asleep in a fire or in deep waters, but he is likely to grow drowsy in the sunshine."

Now let's look at 2 Timothy 4:2, which will summarize the point of this particular chapter. Paul had been writing about the tendency to move away from truth, including the truth of the coming judgment of Christ. Then he wrote in 2 Timothy 4:2-4:

> Preach the word! Be ready in season and out of season. Convince, rebuke, exhort, with all longsuffering and teaching. For the time will come when they will not endure sound doctrine, but according to their own desires, because they have itching ears, they will heap up for themselves teachers; and they will turn their ears away from the truth, and be turned aside to fables.

In essence, Paul said, "Timothy, the reason all of this is happening is that God is coming. The Lord Jesus Christ himself will evaluate you, so preach the Word." He didn't say that we should suggest the Word, or discuss it, or throw our hat in the ring with other philosophies. We should instead preach the Word.

Now I'm not saying we can't discuss with other people their worldviews, but only as we act in love and humility. In Ephesus, Timothy was told to preach. In the Greek language this word "preach" is *karuso*, which means "to proclaim with authority." In Greece, they used this word to describe an imperial messenger or someone who would march through the city streets and announce the news, the policies, new laws of the kingdom, or the appearance of the king. This imperial messenger would act with authority. All of that force is captured in this little word, *preach*. Timothy was motivated to speak out for the Lord Jesus because he was surrounded with a variety of intelligent, persuasive, sophisticated, and gifted orators who were twisting the truth.

Paul was exhorting Timothy before God to preach the Word. And what does it mean "to preach the Word"? This past week I had a discussion with someone about the Word. They said, "Well, that probably just means to preach Jesus or to talk about Jesus. The Word is Jesus. John said so in John 1:1: 'In the beginning was the Word, and the Word was with God.'" Preaching Jesus is definitely part of the message, but to preach the Word means to speak of the true message, the gospel, the Scriptures. Think back to 2 Timothy 2:15. Paul wanted Timothy to put the Word of truth in the front of his mind.

Let's look at these words in context, and follow it through so it will crystallize in our minds. Second Timothy 3:15-4:2 says:

> From childhood you have known the Holy Scriptures, which are able to make you wise for salvation through faith which is in Christ Jesus. All Scripture is given by inspiration of God, and is profitable for doctrine, for reproof, for correction, for instruction in righteousness, that the man of God may be complete, thoroughly equipped for every good work. I charge you therefore before God and the Lord Jesus Christ, who will judge the living and the dead at His appearing and His kingdom. Preach the Word!

What Timothy was to preach is clear. The Word equals Scripture equals doctrine equals truth.

Second Timothy 4:3: "The time will come when they will not endure sound doctrine." I'll discuss this aspect of doctrine more extensively in the next chapter, but the most misunderstood word in the Bible is this word *doctrine*. The word *doctrine* has been beat up and backhanded a great deal, even though Paul seemed to like this word. Back in 2 Timothy

3:16, he said: "All Scripture is given by inspiration of God, and is profitable for doctrine." The Greek word for doctrine is *didaskalia*.[12] In 2 Timothy 4:2, Paul instructed: "Preach the word! Be ready in season and out of season. Convince, rebuke, exhort, with all longsuffering and teaching." Notice this word *didaskalia*, or doctrine, uses the same word as "teaching." And then there is 2 Timothy 4:3: "The time will come when they will not endure sound doctrine." Paul liked the word *doctrine* and used it a great deal.

The word *doctrine* is misunderstood; I know this because of how I hear people use it. They say things like, "I'm not into doctrine; I'm just into Jesus." If you say something like that, it sounds really cool, humble, meek, and hip. Or you will hear someone else say, "I'm not into doctrine because doctrine is so technical, so dogmatic, and so divisive. I'm just into Jesus." The great irony about that statement is that unless you had doctrine, you wouldn't know about Jesus. Doctrine simply means correct, right, healthy teaching.

It's sort of like having a gadget. If you're like me, when I buy a gadget and it comes with a manual, I try not to use it. I don't like the manual. The gadget is cool and sleek, intuitive, and user-friendly, yet the manual is forty times bigger than the gadget. I push the manual aside and forget it is there—until the gadget breaks. Then suddenly I'm asking, "Where's that manual?"

Many people live their lives this way. We are the gadget, and Bible doctrine is the manual. While people don't want to read the Bible, they will carry it around and proclaim, "I own a Bible." Yet they don't follow the manual as any rule of life.

Today, among the majority of Christians, the tendency is to emphasize how you feel, not what is true. When something is said in a Bible study, participants are asked, "How do you feel about that? What does that mean to you?" While it is valid to ask about feelings, these questions should never supersede absolute truth. It's unfortunate, but many people are not seeking the truth. Instead they consider only how they feel about it. God, speaking through the prophet Hosea, said: "My people are destroyed for lack of knowledge" (4:6). We learn in Acts 2: "[The Church] continued steadfastly in the apostles' doctrine" (verse 42). In 1 Timothy 4:13, Paul wrote: "Till I come, give attention to reading, to exhortation, to doctrine." Finally, to Titus, Paul wrote: "Teach what is in accord with sound doctrine" (verse 2:1, NIV).

Several years ago, James Montgomery Boice, who is now in Heaven, wrote these words: "We do not have a strong church today, nor do we have many strong Christians. We can trace the cause to an acute lack of spiritual knowledge. Ask an average Christian to talk about God and after getting past the expected answers, you will find that his God is a little god of vacillating sentiments."[13]

At four different times in the Gospels of the New Testament, Jesus went to the leaders and said, "Have you not read in the Scriptures?" It was as if in the vernacular, Jesus said, "Wait a minute, you men are the scribes and Pharisees, our resident theologians, and you haven't read this material in your Bibles?"

In the Emerging Church, things get a little muddied, and they think the Scripture is not clear. In fact, one of them said, "I don't know if anyone has ever gotten the gospel right." Take a moment and think about that statement. That means the beloved Apostle John didn't get the gospel right, Peter didn't get it right, and Paul didn't get it right. These Emerging Church leaders act as though they've come just in time to let us know and rescue us from all of the ignorance we have endured for two thousand years. If none of us have gotten it right, then we've all been absolutely wrong. They will tell you it's impossible to know absolute truth. In fact, they see a certain virtue in uncertainty. They say you're not *supposed* to know truth; one of their mantras is, "We don't offer answers. We offer mysteries."

This type of teaching is in direct opposition to one of the major tenets of the Protestant Reformation begun under Martin Luther: the perspicuity of Scripture. The word *perspicuity* means "clarity," and it refers to the clear teaching of Scripture. The Scripture is *meant* to be understood, and the central message of the Bible to be plainly seen and plainly interpreted. The Emerging Church leaders say, "God may have spoken, but He mumbled, and we don't exactly know what He said."[14] Tony Jones, one of the leaders of the Emerging Church said, "I'm quite convinced the Bible is a subversive text. I think the Bible is [an expletive that I could never repeat] scary book (pardon my French). I think that deconstruction is the only hermeneutical avenue that comes close to expressing the transgressive nature of the sacred text."[15]

Did that make any sense to you? You are probably saying, "What on Earth does that mean?" That's my point. When I read many of the teachings from these Emerging Church leaders, I pause to say, "Huh?"

I like what someone once said about philosophers, "Philosophers are people who talk about things they don't understand, but they make it sound like it's your fault."[16] I get that same feeling when Tony Jones says, "The only way to get at the true message of the Bible is to deconstruct its traditional message." He's saying that whatever it means, we are confused, and it certainly can't mean what we traditionally thought it did.

In the Emerging Church, the Bible is viewed through the lens of postmodern culture. It means we adapt the teaching of the Scripture through the lens of our culture, rather than seeing our culture through the lens of Scripture. As a result, members of this "church" will never come to any agreement on what is right or wrong, what salvation is, and what sin is. If they don't believe in anything, they can't offend anyone, and that's their whole point.

I will have more to say about this topic in the next chapter, but I want to wrap up this section with these words from my heart. As a pastor, it is my prayer, my hope, my aim, and my purpose to make you the most biblically educated person I can. This is my motivation to plow deeply into the Bible texts. I tell you the meanings of the Greek words and explain the sentence structure because I want you to understand what it says and then apply the meaning to your life. There may be some teachings that you like more than others. When you hear some material you may think, *Who cares about this?* My point is that as I share the Word of God in this book, you will become equipped with absolute truth and get new bearings in your life.

A pastor's wife was going into surgery, and her husband was at her bedside. This woman wasn't sure if she was going to make it through surgery, so she said, "Honey, listen. If I die on the operating table, I want you to know something. First, I love you, and second, there is a shoebox under the bed that holds a secret. There are some things in it I want you to see if I die."

When his wife went into surgery, this pastor couldn't wait. He ran right home and checked under the bed. He pulled out a shoebox that held $10,000—and three eggs. He thought, *This is weird.*

After he returned to the hospital, his wife woke up from surgery and was fine. In the post-op room, the pastor said, "Honey, I love you, and I'm so glad you're out of surgery.

But I saw the shoebox. Help me understand. Why do you have $10,000 and three eggs hidden under the bed?"

"When we first got married," she said, "I was determined not to be a complaining, critical, or nagging spouse. I thought that every time you preached a bad sermon, I'd put one egg in the box and not say anything about it."

At first, he was confused, but then he thought, *Wow, thirty-one years of marriage and only three eggs. That's a pretty good track record!* This pastor was feeling really good about himself.

Then his wife finished her explanation: "Whenever I got a dozen eggs, I'd sell them and put the money in the box."

My point is to be careful what you hear, listen with great discernment, and filter everything through the absolute grid of Scripture. Are there many ambiguous Bible texts? Yes. Are there some things in the Scripture that we don't understand? Absolutely. But the central message of the Bible is clear and understandable. The more we read the Bible and apply it to our daily lives, the firmer our footing will be for the future.

Chapter 9

THE SLIPPERY SLOPE

Picture a blind man standing on the edge of a cliff. As he stands on the edge, he's asking for direction about which way he should go. One step off the cliff could mean his death, but he doesn't exactly know where he is, so he cries out, "Which direction should I go?"

Now you're down below, watching and hearing this blind man. Someone next to you in the crowd shouts to the blind man, "It doesn't matter which way you go, as long as you're sincere!"

What would you tell the man next to you? You'd probably tell him to be quiet! At that point, for the blind man, the right information would be vital. It's not about sincerity; it's about truth.

A memo from a school superintendent to the assistant superintendent said, "Next Thursday morning at 10:30, Halley's Comet will appear over this area. This is an event that occurs only once every seventy-five years. Call the school principals and have them assemble their teachers and classes on their athletic fields and explain this phenomenon to them. If it rains then cancel the classes' observation and have the classes meet in the auditorium to see a film about the comet." That was the original memo from the superintendent to the assistant superintendent.

But the memo from the assistant superintendent to the principals was skewed a bit: "By the order of the superintendent of schools, next Thursday, Halley's Comet will appear over your athletic field. If it rains, then cancel the day's classes and report to the auditorium with your teachers and students where you will be shown films, a phenomenal event that occurs only once every seventy-five years."

Then it passed from the principals to the teachers, and it came out this way: "By the order of the phenomenal superintendent of schools, at 10:30 on Thursday, Halley's Comet will appear in the auditorium. In the case of rain over the athletic field, the superintendent will give another order, something which occurs only once every seventy-five years."

Then it passed from the teachers to the students, and it came out this way: "Next Thursday at 10:30, the superintendent of schools will appear in our school auditorium with Halley's Comet, something which occurs only once every seventy-five years. If it rains, the superintendent will cancel the comet and will order us out to our phenomenal athletic field."

Finally the students told the parents: "When it rains next Thursday at 10:30 over the school athletic field, the phenomenal seventy-five-year-old superintendent of the schools will cancel all classes and appear before the school in the auditorium accompanied by Bill Hailey and the Comets."

When information leaves its original source, its accuracy can rapidly deteriorate. Each time it is repeated, its reliability can be skewed. Anyone who teaches the Bible and preaches the truth must make sure that what they speak is as close to the original message as is possible.

Years ago the ministry of Charles Hadden Spurgeon, a name you have likely heard many times, was active during the Victorian Era in London, England. For the last four years of his life, Spurgeon was embroiled in a controversy known as the downgrade controversy. Charles Spurgeon warned England, his church, and the union of which he was a part, about the slippery slope of moving away from the truth. Spurgeon compared historic Christianity to the pinnacle of a mountain; if you took one step in the wrong direction, then you would be on the slippery slope.

In the last chapter, we touched on some of the issues regarding our need to see the truth. I mentioned the Emerging Church movement, which is on the rise, and the World Council of Churches, which has been around for a long time promoting liberalism and relativism.

The real problem is not the Emerging Church, or the World Council of Churches, or even liberalism itself. These elements are just symptoms of the real problem: the demand that creates the supply. It is our wants, our values, what we determine to be most important, that creates the supply. Do we want pure truth, or do we just want to feel good about ourselves? When Paul wrote to Timothy, the Church was already on the slippery slope. First and Second Timothy contain enough language to indicate the Christians at Ephesus had fallen away from the truth.

Another element was present in this situation that I want to discuss. The church at Ephesus was facing persecution unlike they had ever known before. Second Timothy was probably written about A.D. 67. A few years before this letter was written, in A.D. 64, a huge fire destroyed large portions of the city of Rome. Some people said that the emperor Nero lit this fire himself. But Nero wanted a scapegoat for the fire, so he blamed the Christians who were already viewed negatively in the eyes of society. This finger pointing at the Christians spawned a series of persecutions. In Rome, believers were killed en masse, facing horrific deaths that had not occurred before this time.

Now this persecution of the Christians was starting to spill into other parts of the empire. Because Christians wanted to be less visible, they wanted to soften their message. Instead of stepping up to the plate with the gospel message, they wanted to take a lower profile. When Paul wrote to young Timothy, he was contending, "Timothy, listen. God placed you in Ephesus. This is not the time to tone down your message. If anything, now is the time to increase your efforts and preach the Word."

As Christians, we are called to proclaim the truth, In 2 Timothy 4:2, Paul wrote: "Preach the word!" Second Timothy 3:16 defines that "word" as the Scriptures that God has given. If Timothy was called to speak the truth, it was because his hearers were called to know the truth. This speaking and knowing is mandated in the Scriptures, despite what we hear from leaders in the Emerging Church movement. They say, "We're in postmodern America, and you can't really know for certain what is truth. If you say you know the truth, you've taken a very arrogant position." As I've studied the teaching of these leaders, I've learned their only acceptable "religion" is to say, "It doesn't matter what you believe. As long as you're sincere, you can believe anything you want." "Sincerity above doctrine" is their mantra.

Imagine you go to the doctor and he diagnoses you with a malignant tumor. In shock, you say, "Doctor, what should I do?"

The doctor says, "You could go home, kick up your feet, and watch television all day. Or I could operate on it. Either way it doesn't matter, as long as you're sincere."

You'd say, "Excuse me, doctor, but you sound like a quack!"

Paul noticed there were spiritual "quacks" in Ephesus who were giving such life-destroying wrong direction to people.

In a Christian school, a teacher once asked the students to take a test that wasn't written; it was a verbal test. As she asked the questions, the students were to write down their answers. "First question," the teacher said. "What is false doctrine?"

To the ears of one little boy, the word *doctrine* sounded like *doctoring*. So he wrote, "False doctrine is when a doctor gives the wrong stuff to people who are sick." That's actually a good definition, even for the biblical sense of false doctrine.

In the last chapter, I told you that in Greek the word *preach*, or *kerusso*,[1] means an authoritative proclamation. The leaders in the Emerging Church say there is no way to proclaim with authority, so they call it a "conversation." They say, "Let's have a dialogue, or a conversation. We'll never really come to the knowledge of the truth, but we can have an interesting conversation about it."

Consider the Ten Commandments. Was that a conversation? No! You couldn't even call it a dialogue because it was a monologue. God revealed His Word through the Commandments. When Jesus Christ gave the Sermon on the Mount, it wasn't a conversation, either. That was a monologue in which Jesus spoke about how to live in the kingdom.

When the prophets said, "Thus saith the LORD," it wasn't a conversation. Or when Paul wrote his letters, such as

Timothy or Galatians or Ephesians, it wasn't a conversation. It was the revealed Word of the Lord, or the truth for those churches. Now think back to a *conversation* between Satan and Eve in the Garden of Eden. That didn't turn out very well! When you preach the Word, it denotes absolute truth.

Second Timothy 4:2 continues: "Be ready in season and out of season." You could translate that as Paul saying, "Timothy, whether it's convenient or inconvenient, whether it's in season and tolerated or out of season and not tolerated, preach the Word." Let's face it, these days preaching the Word of God is out of season because experts say it is too isolating, rigid, and authoritative.

Notice that Paul told Timothy what tone to use when preaching the Word: "Convince, rebuke, exhort, with all longsuffering and teaching" (verse 2). Of these three words— *convince, rebuke,* and *exhort*—the first two are negative and the third is positive. To *convince* means to correct misbehavior or false doctrine, while to *rebuke* means to bring someone to repentance. But *exhort* means to encourage, help along, or instruct with gentleness. Paul told young Timothy to be tough yet tender in his tone and balance both positive and negative elements together.

When I preach, sometimes people will write notes to me the following week. One young man suggested, "I think you should focus more on the positive teachings of Jesus." I understand this desire to look for the positive. When I read that note, I smiled and thought about what the well-known pastor and teacher Stuart Briscoe used to say to young ministers. Dr. Briscoe said, "Here's the qualification for being a pastor: You need the mind of a scholar, the heart of a child, and the hide of a rhinoceros." If I'm really frank with you—not arrogant but honest—I don't care what anyone thinks about what I preach except for one—and that's God.

Isn't that the way we ought to live? God loves you the way you are, but He loves you too much to leave you the way you are. Whenever we read the truth, it will confront us with some area where we need to change. We have a mandate to preach the Word in a tone that is convincing, rebuking, and exhorting.

Second Timothy 4:3-4 tells us the consequences of neglecting the truth. Paul was predicting the future with these verses: "For the time will come when they will not endure sound doctrine, but according to their own desires, because they have itching ears, they will heap up for themselves teachers; and they will turn their ears away from the truth, and be turned aside to fables." Notice how Paul made these types of statements several different places in the New Testament. He would be speaking about something in the present, then he would move into speaking about the future to warn people to be ready.

For example, Paul made this transition in Acts 20. He gathered together the elders in Ephesus, the same church where Timothy was the pastor. Then he said, "I know this, that after my departure savage wolves will come in among you, not sparing the flock. Also from among yourselves men will rise up, speaking perverse things, to draw away the disciples after themselves" (verses 29-30). In 1 Timothy 4:1, he wrote: "Now the Spirit expressly says that in latter times some will depart from the faith, giving heed to deceiving spirits and doctrines of demons" (or demonically inspired teaching). And in 2 Timothy 3:1 he wrote: "Know this, that in the last days perilous times will come," and there's a whole list in that description, among which he wrote: "[They'll have] a form of godliness but denying its power" (verse 5).

In 2 Timothy 4:3-4 Paul predicted: "They will not endure sound doctrine." Have you ever considered how to endure sound doctrine? The other night, I was reading Charles Spurgeon's *Lectures to My Students*, which was a book he wrote to young ministers. His chapter on praying said: "When you're praying publicly in front of your congregation, before your sermon, you want to make sure that your prayer is no longer than ten minutes or maybe fifteen minutes. Only on rare occasions should it ever go up to twenty minutes." He was talking about the prayer *before* the sermon!

In many places today, twenty-minute sermons aren't tolerated, let alone ten-minute prayers. Regarding this tendency to speak for a shorter period of time, Charles Spurgeon wrote: "Everywhere there is apathy. Nobody cares whether that which is preached is true or false. A sermon is a sermon, whatever the subject, only the shorter it is, the better."[2]

In many congregations if you were to announce, "Hey, we're going to cut the preaching in half and we're going to have more music," your decision would be applauded. In 2 Timothy 4:3-4, the Apostle Paul foresaw a time when truth would be eclipsed by novelty and cleverness. We believe this letter was the aging apostle's last before his death. He made an interesting prediction.

During 2004, at an Emerging Church conference, the leaders got together and composed this statement: "Preaching," they said, "is broken, too authoritative and rigid." Paul predicted this season when he wrote, "For the time will come when they will not endure sound doctrine." The Greek word for "sound" is *hugianos*, from which we get the words *hygiene* and *hygienic*. It means clean, pure, healthy, safe and sound doctrine.

Paul was giving a description of someone who turns away from feeding on the truth to snacking on substitutes. They won't endure sound doctrine because they want something different. In Ephesians 4:14, Paul wrote: "That we should no longer be children, tossed to and fro and carried about with every wind of doctrine, by the trickery of men, in the cunning craftiness of deceitful plotting." Instead of turning to substitutes, we need to feed on pure healthy food.

I read about a farmer who complained about the rising cost of oats, just like we complain about the increase in the price of gasoline. This farmer bought oats for his mules. He decided to substitute sawdust for some of the mule's oats. Each day, he took out a little more oats and substituted more sawdust to wean the mules off the oats. By the time the mules were satisfied with the sawdust instead of oats, they were dead. Here's my point: You can snack on substitutes rather than feed on the truth of the Scriptures, but it is spiritually detrimental. We need to preach the Word, the truth, because the time is coming when people won't put up with the truth.

Years ago, A. W. Tozer wrote:

> It is scarcely possible in most places to get anyone to attend a meeting where the only attraction is God. One can only conclude that God's professed children are bored with him for they must be wooed to meetings with a stick of striped candy in the form of religious movies, games and refreshments.

Here's my question: Why would anyone turn away from sound, healthy, safe teaching? The answer is found in 2 Timothy 4:3 with the little phrase "own desires": "The time will come when they will not endure sound doctrine, but according to their own desires." In other words, these people will look for someone to tell them what they want to hear.

In the Old Testament, the prophet Isaiah was the spokesperson to the nation of Israel. Isaiah 30:10 says:

145

"[They] say to the seers, 'Do not see,' and to the prophets, 'Do not prophesy to us right things; speak to us smooth things, prophesy deceits.'" You know the truth isn't always smooth. The truth doesn't always tickle the ears, but sometimes it first boxes the ears, and *then* it brings comfort.

Peter preached in the Book of Acts, and "they were cut to the heart" (2:37). When Jesus preached in John 6: "Many of His disciples went back and walked with Him no more" (verse 66). Now understand, often people don't instantly turn away from the truth. Most of the time, it doesn't happen overnight, but it is a process. It takes time, but Paul was writing Timothy only a little over thirty years after Jesus walked the Earth—which isn't all that long.

As a modern example, when the Pilgrim forefathers landed in this country, they built churches, homes, and schools. After they completed the churches and homes, they thought, *Now we need to educate our children*, so they built a school, and with its name, they honored one of their pastors, John Harvard. Harvard University had the sole purpose to train ministers to preach the gospel. Today, if you look at Harvard, see if you can find a preacher of the gospel. Yes, the school has a theological school, but examine their literature and you will find how far from its roots this school has come.

John Harvard said, "We are dreading to leave an illiterate ministry to the churches when our present ministers shall lie in the dust." They developed an original crest for Harvard University that included a saying combined with three books; one of the books faced downward. Above the books, the Latin words were written, *Veritas Christo et Ecclesiae*,[3] or "truth for Christ and the Church." Those words were the original motto for Harvard University. One of the three books faced down to symbolize the limitation of human knowledge. Today's Harvard University crest is different from the original. All three books are facing upward to show the unlimited capacity of the human mind. The Latin motto has been reduced to one word from the original sentence: *veritas*, which is the word for "truth." Harvard continues to pursue truth, but the involvement of Christ and the Church is long gone. Where Harvard began and where it ended up are miles apart.

In 2 Timothy 4:5-8, we are commanded to nurture the truth. Paul wrote:

> But you be watchful in all things, endure afflictions, do the work of an evangelist, fulfill [completely accomplish] your ministry. For I am already being poured out as a drink offering, and the time of my departure is at hand. I have fought the good fight, I have finished the race, I have kept the faith. Finally, there is laid up for me the crown of righteousness, which the Lord, the righteous Judge, will give to me on that Day, and not to me only but also to all who have loved His appearing. (Words in brackets added.)

Notice how Paul began verse 5, because it's a contrast: "But you, [Timothy]." He was saying, "In contrast to those who neglect the truth, you, Timothy, stand firm in the truth and nurture the truth."

Paul used his own life as an example. This aging apostle was writing from a Roman prison toward the end of his life. With satisfaction Paul could say, "In the grace of Christ I have finished the race, I have kept the faith." Our calling is to believe the truth, our calling is to love the truth, and our calling is to speak the truth. There are times when I read the Bible and I say, "I love that verse; it is so comforting to me."

Yet that doesn't always happen. Sometimes I read a verse and I say, "Uh-oh, I remember that verse. That kind of hurts."

I want you to permit yourself to have either experience when you read the Scriptures. Let the truth confront you as well as comfort you. Let the truth hurt you as well as heal you. Someone once said, "The Scripture was written to comfort the afflicted and to afflict the comfortable."[4]

I love to preach about the love of God, the grace of God, the mercy of Christ, and our riches as believers. Each of us loves those truths, and they must be safeguarded and defended, not abandoned. But we cannot roll over and just say, "Oh well, think good, positive thoughts and the controversy over truth will go away." It won't.

Remember that little book of Jude in the New Testament? Verse 3 says: "Contend earnestly for the faith which was once for all delivered to the saints." It doesn't mean to *be contentious* for the faith, but to *contend* for the faith. "For certain men have crept in unnoticed" (verse 4). We must notice when they creep in.

Let me conclude this chapter by saying I do see light at the end of this tunnel. With the surge of postmodernism, with the rise of the Emerging Church, with the wholesale denial of any absolute truth, do you know what happens? People are left disillusioned, confused, and groping for answers. We have a great opportunity to step into those situations where people want to know the truth. We can help them with love, humility, and *certainty*, because we can tell them the truth. Hebrews 1:1-2 says: "God, who at various times and in various ways spoke in time past to the fathers by the prophets, has in these last days spoken to us by His Son." I'll give you this warning: If you love the truth, and you stand up for it, and you preach the Gospel of Jesus Christ, in this age of tolerance, you won't be tolerated. They'll tolerate everything else and anything else except your message. Be ready for that.

Here's the question: Will you live to please men or will you live to please the Father? Understand, you are not going to face other people in eternity, but Him.

Years ago, a letter was written to *The British Weekly*, a newspaper in England. They published this snide letter in the newspaper, which began, "Dear Sir, I noticed that ministers seem to set a great deal of importance on their sermons and spend a great deal of time in preparing them. I've been attending services quite regularly for the past thirty years, and during that time, if I estimate correctly, I've listened to no less than three thousand sermons. But to my consternation I've discovered I cannot remember a single one of them. I wonder if a minister's time might be more profitably spent on something else." And he signed it.

Most people have that feeling about sermons and think, *Why did you spend so much time on that?* This letter in the newspaper created a furor of letter activity with pros and cons written back and forth. Finally the paper received the ultimate rebuttal: "My dear sir, I've been married for thirty years. During that time I have eaten 32,850 meals, mostly my wife's cooking. Suddenly I've discovered that I cannot remember the menu of a single meal. And yet I've received nourishment from every one of them. I have the distinct impression that without them I would have starved to death long ago." And he signed it.

As we secure our souls, our families, our relationships, and our moral lives, let's make sure the Church is secure as well. Don't be afraid to raise that flag of discernment. Don't be afraid to compare it with the Scripture to find "whether these things were so" (Acts 17:11, KJV). That makes for a vital, vibrant, healthy, strong Church.

Chapter 10

ABRAHAM'S OTHER SON

On June 8, A.D. 632, Mohammed, the founder of Islam, died and was buried in Medina. Each year hundreds of thousands visit his tomb, not to celebrate a resurrection but simply a life and a death.

Many years ago a Muslim and a Christian were having a conversation and the Muslim said, "Look, at least we Muslims go to Medina and we can look at a coffin. You Christians go to Jerusalem, and all you see is an empty grave."

The Christian smiled and said, "Yeah, that's the whole point." The fact of the Resurrection is what separates Jesus from every other religion.

E. Stanley Jones, a Christian missionary to India, said, "The Buddhist and the Hindu stand aside disillusioned. The Muslim submits. But only the Christian exults." In the pages of this chapter and the next, I want to examine the religion of Islam from two different perspectives: first the threat of Islam, and second, the opportunity for Christians to witness to this group of people.

The Department of Homeland Security was founded, in large part, as a response to the threat of radical Islam against the United States. But this book doesn't consider this as just a threat. Instead, we can view radical Islam as one of the greatest opportunities of the present day. After all, Jesus loves the Muslim people, and He died on the cross for them, too. As much as possible, we want to reach out to them for Jesus Christ.

I'm going to use Genesis 16 to approach the topic of Islam through the life of Ishmael, the other son of Abraham. In the Old Testament, Isaac was the predominant son of Abraham. He was the son of promise born to Abraham and his wife, Sarah. Ishmael was the other son of Abraham. By the way, Abraham had six other sons with his second wife, Keturah. I'm aware that not all Muslims trace their ethnic lineage back to Ishmael. Yet all Muslims will trace their spiritual heritage back to Abraham through Ishmael. They regard Ishmael to be a prophet, and he is mentioned in the Koran. I believe the religion of Islam has enabled the Arab peoples to see a fulfillment of some of the predictions we're going to read about in this chapter.

Where did the earthly hatred of Israel originate? Why has that rift been there for so long, and why has the conflict in the Middle East placed the world on the brink of global war for so many years? Where did that all begin, what is the agenda in that part of the world, and was any of it foreseen in the Scriptures? In the next few pages, we're going to look at four elements: Ishmael's birth, his predicted numbers, the significance of his name, and finally his nature.

Let's examine Genesis 16: 1-3 and learn about the birth of Ishmael:

Now Sarai [that was Sarah's name before her name was changed], Abram's wife [Abram was Abraham's name before it was changed], had borne him no children. And she had an Egyptian maidservant whose name was Hagar. So Sarai said to Abram, "See now, the LORD has restrained me from bearing children. Please, go in to my maid; perhaps I shall obtain children by her." And Abram heeded the voice of Sarai. Then Sarai, Abram's wife, took Hagar her maid, the Egyptian, and gave her to her husband Abram to be his wife, after Abram had dwelt ten years in the land of Canaan. (Words in brackets added.)

You may have heard the old saying, "God helps those who help themselves." My dad used to quote it, saying, "The Bible says, 'God helps those who help themselves.'" But when I read the Bible, I discovered this saying was not in any version of the Bible. Jesus never said those words, nor did any of the apostles any or other writers of the Bible! It's a "phantom verse." Actually, the opposite of the saying is true. The Bible says that God helps those who *can't* help themselves, because that's what redemption is all about. In this story about Ishmael, we see the case of Sarah and Abraham trying to help God so He can fulfill His promise.

In the days of Abraham, it was horrible to be childless in any society. Eleven years before, God had promised this couple that they would have a child, but for eleven years they waited with no results.

I imagine a conversation went something like this, "Abe, honey, I know you really want me to have a child, but come on, look at me. I'm seventy-five years old, and it's not going happen." The couple came up with a plan to help God fulfill His promise of a child. As you read through this chapter, it's easy to see that Abraham was not exactly a Rock of Gibraltar when it came to exhibiting strength. Abraham was passive throughout this whole series of events.

Abraham looked at Sarah and said, "Okay, now let me understand, Sarah. You want me to have sexual relations with your maid? And you're okay with that, and believe that's God's will? Well, okay, if you insist. Someone's got to sacrifice, so I guess I'll do it!"

Now you should understand that societal codes of the day made it legal for a wife who couldn't bear a child to use a servant as a surrogate mother. When this servant bore her child, she gave it the name of that couple and it was perfectly legal. But just because something is legal in a society, it isn't necessarily biblical.

For example, it is legal to divorce your spouse for irreconcilable differences, yet it's not biblical to do so. It's legal to have an abortion, yet it's not biblical to do so. It's legal to get drunk, yet it's not biblical to do so. The issue here isn't what the court allows; your focus should be on what God allows.

Abraham and Sarah's plan to help God backfired. Genesis 16:4-5 says: "So he went in to Hagar, and she conceived. And when she saw that she had conceived, her mistress became despised in her eyes. Then Sarai said to Abram, 'My wrong be upon you! I gave my maid into your embrace, and when she saw that she had conceived, I became despised in her eyes. [See how she twisted this whole thing?] The LORD judge between you and me'" (words in brackets added). Abraham's wife, Sarah, became very jealous and angry, and she blamed her husband.

Now notice how Abraham responded. Genesis 16:6 says: "So Abram said to Sarai, 'Indeed your maid is in your hand; do to her as you please.' And when Sarai dealt harshly with her, she fled from her presence." Once again Abram's response was very passive: "Whoa, woman, back off. You handle this." Many men give this type of response today: "I don't want to handle it, so you take care of it."

Next Sarai knocked Hagar down from concubine status to once again become a slave, which again, according to the ancient codes, was perfectly legal. Genesis 16:7-10 says:

> Now the Angel of the LORD found her by a spring of water in the wilderness, by the spring on the way to Shur. And He said, "Hagar, Sarai's maid, where have you come from, and where are you going?" She said, "I am fleeing from the presence of my mistress Sarai." The Angel of the LORD said to her, "Return to your mistress, and submit yourself under her hand." Then the Angel of the LORD said to her, "I will multiply your descendants exceedingly, so that they shall not be counted for multitude."

While Sarai and Abram rejected this woman, Hagar, God did not reject her. Instead, God sent the angel of the Lord to comfort, console, direct, and instruct Hagar. By the way, this occurrence of "the Angel of the LORD" is the first mention of this unique person in the Old Testament. Who is the angel of the Lord? There is no clear-cut answer to this question. Some people say it's a lower angel, while others contend it is some greater level of angel. The Muslims say that perhaps this angel of the Lord was the angel Gabriel. And some other commentators say that this angel is a preincarnate form of Jesus Christ in the Old Testament (including the translators of the New King James Version, which I am using in this book). This holds credence because the angel speaks in the first-person tense, as though God himself was speaking. Also, the phrase "the angel of the Lord" appears throughout the Old Testament, but these appearances suddenly stop after the birth of Christ.

Within Islam, angels are very important. In fact, Islam has a whole angelic hierarchy that stretches from Allah down to mankind. Of course, in Islam, the most important angel is Gabriel because Gabriel appeared to Mohammed the prophet and gave him the various revelations. Islam also says that every single human being has two angels that follow him: one keeps a record of all the person's good deeds and one records the bad. Then, on the Day of Judgment, the records of the two angels are reviewed.

Focus on the language of Genesis 16:9: "The Angel of the LORD said to her, 'Return to your mistress, and submit yourself under her hand.'" Within Islam, a key concept is submission. In fact, the word *Islam* means "submission," and the word *Muslim* means "one who submits." When the angel instructed Hagar, "Go submit," according to Muslim tradition, Hagar did not do that, which I'll explain in just a moment.

Islamic tradition traces Islam as a religion back to Abraham. They believe Abraham, their father, submitted to the will of Allah and gave them the religion of Islam. They say, "This is the religion of your father, Abraham; he called you *Muslim* or 'those who submit to the will of Allah.'" But according to Muslim tradition, Hagar did not return to Abraham and Sarah and submit; instead, she fled to Saudi Arabia. Also, according to the Islam tradition, Abraham left Sarah by herself and followed Hagar with Ishmael to Saudi Arabia. Further, they say Abraham and his son Ishmael built the Kaaba, which is the big black stone they say is the center of the universe and which currently rests inside their grand mosque in Mecca.

Now let's look at Genesis 16:10, which provides a prediction of the numbers that are to follow: "The Angel of the Lord said to her, 'I will multiply your descendants exceedingly, so that they shall not be counted for multitude." The majority of Arabs trace their lineage back to Ishmael. Today, among the Arab states, there is a population of 325 million people, which includes twenty-two countries that span two different continents. The majority of those countries fall under the banner of Islam. In fact, 20 percent of the world's population is Muslim, and Islam is the second largest religion in the world, with 1.3 billion followers. Take that in for a moment: One out of every five people on planet Earth is a Muslim, and Islam's numbers are growing and spreading worldwide.[1]

Let's frame these statistics in modern terms. In 1945, there was one mosque in the entire nation of England. Today there are thousands upon thousands, and hundreds of those mosques were churches that have been converted into mosques. In fact, the same church that sent out William Carey, who is known as the father of modern-day missions within the Christian Church, has been converted into a mosque. In China there are 100 million Muslims, in Indonesia 180 million, and they all relate spiritually back to Ishmael. Currently the United States of America has about three thousand mosques. In 1990, how many mosques were in America? Thirty. They say every single week in the United States, a new mosque opens, and already an Islamic leader has inaugurated a session of the United States Senate by praying in the name of Allah.[2]

Saudi Arabia and other countries pour in tens of millions of dollars each year to spread the faith of Islam, throughout the United States in particular. This spread of Islam is an example of how your oil dollars are put to work. In fact, the

Muslim strategists often say, "Why is it that Allah has blessed our country with all of the wealth of the oil of the world if not for this reason?" In Dearborn, Michigan, one imam said, "Just as you send Christian missionaries to subSahara Africa, we are spreading our faith in America." In America, they claim 2,500 converts to Islam every day.[3]

Look at Genesis 16:11 and consider the name of Ishmael: "The Angel of the LORD said to her, 'Behold, you are with child, and you shall bear a son. You shall call his name Ishmael, because the LORD has heard your affliction.'" The name *Ishmael* means "the Lord will hear," or "the Lord will heed." This is not a name Hagar created, nor did she use the *1001 Baby Names* book. The angel of the Lord gave Hagar the name for her child. Genesis 16:13-16 says:

> Then she called the name of the LORD who spoke to her, You-are-the-God-who-sees; for she said, "Have I also here seen Him who sees me?" Therefore the well was called Beer Lahai Roi; observe, it is between Kadesh and Bered. So Hagar bore Abram a son; and Abram named his son, whom Hagar bore, Ishmael. Abram was eighty-six years old when Hagar bore Ishmael to Abram.

According to the Koran, in Surah 19:54, Ishmael was a prophet and an apostle. (A *surah* is a chapter; the Koran contains 114 chapters, or surahs.) Ishmael is mentioned twelve times in the Koran. Remember, Abraham loved his son because he was his own flesh and blood. Abraham didn't despise his son Ishmael; he loved him. In fact, Abraham had such love for Ishmael that he mentioned him to God in Genesis 17, when God said, "Abraham, Sarah, I'm still going to give you a son miraculously, it's going to be Isaac."

Abraham said, "Oh, that Ishmael might live before you. Just fulfill your promise through him. Make it easy." Abraham loved him.

In Genesis 25 we learn that Ishmael had twelve sons. We often recall Abraham, Isaac, Jacob, and his twelve sons, who initiated the twelve tribes of Israel. But be aware that Ishmael also had twelve sons who also populated that part of the world, and many Arabs today claim Ishmael as their ancestor.

The angel of the Lord predicted Ishmael's nature in Genesis 16:12: "He shall be a wild man; his hand shall be against every man, and every man's hand against him, And he shall dwell in the presence of all his brethren." Notice this verse includes different phrases of description. At first, Ishmael is described as fiercely independent, or "a wild man." The literal Hebrew, which is not adequately translated here, means "he shall be a wild donkey of a man." This phrase is not intended as a slur but as a compliment. In that period of history, one of the most respected animals was the desert onager,[4] or wild donkey. This animal didn't need anyone, could live off the land, and was autonomous, mobile, and fiercely independent. In Job 39, God himself described the wild donkey as one of His prize creations. The sons of Ishmael were described as this revered animal, which is very mobile and lives off the land. If you study the history of the sons of Ishmael, from the time of Abraham until today, one group of these people is known as the Bedouins, who live in tents. Today, 10 percent of the population of the central Middle East is still Bedouin. They live in tents, shun the cities, live off the land, possess herds of animals, and migrate from place to place according to the rainfall patterns. Many times, I've sat in a Bedouin tent and held long discussions with some of the tribal leaders. The men do all the "important work," drink coffee all day long, and talk about life, while the women do the "little things" like watering and feeding all the flocks and all the other work in their culture. While the men discuss the important things of life, they'll give you cup after cup of coffee. They live very basic lives (I say this tongue-in-cheek because I've seen some Bedouin tents with television antennas poking out of the top! It's funny to see these tents in the wilderness where they are living off the land but think one of the basic necessities is television.)

But Genesis 16:12 implies a firm defiance rising in Ishmael: "His hand shall be against every man, and every man's hand against him." While these words are fairly straightforward, in case you have any doubt, listen to the explanation from two of the foremost scholars of the Old Testament, who said, "These words describe the incessant state of feud (or war) with each other and with their neighbors. Here's what it means. The prediction is a group of people who will be fighting each other and fighting their neighbors."

Islam has enabled this group of people to fulfill this particular passage. Not only are some of the radicals against the whole world, and especially the West, but the Sunnis are fighting the Shiites in very bloody conflicts. This situation begs the question: Is Islam a peaceful religion?

There are many spin doctors who would love to say nothing but peaceful things about Islam because they have a vested interest in doing so. But is it really peaceful? The origin of Islam paints a different picture from those who want you to believe it is a wonderful, peaceful religion. To give you a thumbnail sketch, in A.D. 570, Mohammed was born in the city of Mecca. Later on he married a wealthy widow, Hadijah, his first wife, and he had eleven additional wives. This wealthy widow whom Mohammed married was fifteen years his senior. Because of her money, Mohammed had a lot of time on his hands to get very contemplative. He'd go out to the desert for days, which stretched to weeks and then up to a month, thinking and contemplating. In the year A.D. 610 on Mount Herah, in a cave, Mohammed purportedly for the first time received a revelation from God, through the angel Gabriel. During this first encounter, the angel Gabriel told Mohammed to recite the name of God. By the way, *Koran* means "a recital," in which words are recited in a dictation form. The Koran claims to be the words of God that were recited to Mohammed.

Mohammed was told to recite the name of Allah, but he didn't do it; he just listened. Because Mohammed was sitting there unresponsive, the angel insisted, until finally, according to Mohammed, the angel grabbed him by the throat and almost killed him until he recited the name of God. Subsequent revelations followed.

Afterward, Mohammed went to Mecca and began telling the people to turn away from polytheism, the worship of many gods, and to worship Allah, the one god. He warned them that God's judgment would come to them. The people didn't receive the warning very well and persecuted him, which forced Mohammed to flee Mecca and move to a town that later on became known as Medina. When Mohammed gained enough strength and armed men, he used the sword to force the residents of Medina and Mecca to convert to Islam. Mohammed himself personally engaged in forty-seven battles. This armed action stands in direct contrast to the words of the Lord Jesus Christ, who said, "Whoever slaps you on your right cheek, turn the other to him also" (Matthew 5:39).

The prophet Mohammed personally oversaw the slaughter of hundreds of people in the Medina marketplace. Muslims have well-documented Mohammed's violent behavior. One of Mohammed's earliest biographers, a man named Ibn Ishaq[5] and a devout Muslim, wrote: "The apostle of Allah [that's what they called Mohammed] sat with his companions and they were brought to him in small groups between 600 and 700 in number and their heads were struck off, although some will put the figure as high as between 800 and 900." This description is about the founder of Islam, whose dying words were, "O Lord, perish the Jews and the Christians. Beware there should be no two faiths in Arabia." In contrast, among Jesus' last words were: "Father, forgive them, they don't know what they're doing" (see Luke 23:34), or, "Into your hands I commit my spirit" (see Luke 23:46). There is an obvious reason that Islam calls Mohammed the prophet of the sword.

What does the Islamic holy book teach about this behavior of Mohammed? Is the Koran a peaceful book? I've read the Koran, and in Islam there is no redeemer. There is no mediator, nor are there any guarantees of salvation. In the Koran one verse in every 7.9 speaks about or threatens hell, as compared to the Old Testament, where hell is mentioned only in one verse among every 722. In the New Testament, hell is mentioned only in one verse among every 120. The Koran includes 109 verses on war, which accounts for one out of every 55 verses in the Koran. The most famous war verse is called the "verse of the sword," known as *Ayat al-Sayf*, Surah chapter 9 verse 5: "When the forbidden months are past [that's Ramadan] then fight and slay the pagans wherever you find them and seize them, beleaguer them and lie in wait for them in every stratagem of war."

I realize there are many peace-loving, moderate Muslims, but that is because they are moderate or liberal. If they're fundamental Muslims, it's a different case because the Islamic religion and its history are certainly not peaceful. Radical

Muslims will cite the verse of the sword as justification to kill people in Jerusalem by a suicide bomber wearing explosives. According to Islam, the whole world is divided into two groups of people: one group is called *Dar al-Islam*, or the House of Islam, which includes all those who submit to Allah. The second group is called *Dar al-harb*, or the House of War. I doubt that you or I are included in the House of Islam.

The final prediction made about Ishmael is found in Genesis 16:12: "And he shall dwell in the presence of all his brethren." Literally this phrase means, "he shall dwell over against his brethren." There are two interpretations of the exact meaning of this phrase. Some commentators believe it literally means he will dwell to the East against them. The Ishmaelites originally settled to the east of the nation of Israel. This phrase could also mean the Ishmaelites will dwell in the face of Israel. Either interpretation of the phrase is true because a large population of Arabic peoples live to the east, and no matter where they live in the face of the nation of Israel, they have a strong dislike, to put it mildly, for the Jewish nation.

A Lebanese woman, Brigitte Gabriel,[6] grew up in a Muslim community and wrote a book called *Because They Hate: A Survivor of Islamic Terror Warns America.*[7] When Gabriel was growing up, this is what she heard: "The only time we will have peace in the Middle East is to kill all the Jews and throw them into the sea."[8]

Muslim children are learning to hate. In school, Arab children are taught to chant and sing just as our children sing innocent little songs. But listen to the chilling words Arab children are taught: "Arabs are beloved; Jews are dogs; Jews, your blood is kosher to us."[9] Imagine instilling that message into the heart and the mind of a little child to be sung as a nursery rhyme in school!

The government of Saudi Arabia also supplies curriculum to different people throughout the Middle East. These books are teaching the children to become suicide bombers. Part of the eighth-grade curriculum says: "Jews and Christians are apes and pigs; Allah has cursed them."[10]

At this point, you are probably thinking *Skip, you are really citing Muslim extremists*. Well, yes and no. No, in that I'm giving you the origins of Islam, which are factual and historical, so anyone could locate this information. And yes, for a moment, let's say I've only selected the extremists in these recent examples. Let's say it's all peace-loving except just a small percentage. But what is that percentage? Some people would guess maybe 10 percent, which would equal 130 million radical Islamic extremists.

But let's not guess that 10 percent would be radical, and instead follow the more conservative thinking of Hosni Mubarak of Egypt, Musharraf of Pakistan, King Fahd of Saudi Arabia, or Abdullah of King Jordan. These moderates say, "Of all the Muslims in the world, there is at best, one percent who are radical, or only thirteen million."

For a moment, think about *thirteen million people* who believe the United States is the Great Satan and must be destroyed at all costs. What were only *twenty* of them able to accomplish on September 11, 2001? You may be thinking, "Why do these people think this way? Why would they want to kill themselves to harm us?" These radical extremists think this way because Muslim theology contains an important encouragement for suicide bombing and attacks. These attacks are based on the doctrine of *abrogation* (to be discussed in our next chapter). Until you come to grips with this Islamic doctrine, you will never understand the mind of a radical Muslim.

I want to conclude this chapter on a positive note, because I believe that rather than seeing the threat, we should see the opportunity. Here's just one incident that has been multiplied many times over in the Middle East. A devout Kuwaiti Muslim, Ebrahim (Abraham), became wealthy through the television production business. He made several sacred pilgrimages to Mecca, started studying the Koran, and became very interested in spiritual things. But the more he studied the Koran, and despite his various pilgrimages, he lacked peace in his life, and he tried to commit suicide four different times.

One year during the month of Ramadan, he was traveling in England and couldn't sleep. In his sleeplessness, Ebrahim found a Gideon Bible, which he took out and began to read. The Bible directed him to Psalm 4 if he couldn't sleep. Psalm 4:8 says: "I will both lie down in peace, and sleep; for You alone, O LORD, make me dwell in safety." Ebrahim looked up and said, "If you're the God of this book, then give me sleep." Ebrahim sprawled on his bed and went right into a sound sleep for the rest of the night. Throughout the week Ebrahim met several Christian women. He was resistant to their message at first, yet by the end of that week, he prayed to receive Jesus Christ.

While Ebrahim's family rejected his life-changing decision to follow Jesus Christ, you can't imagine the fallout. He married a Christian woman and his family disowned him. Recently he heard from his father, who said, "I know your God is real, because for ten years all of our plans to harm you have failed." This story about Ebrahim is one example of many conversions to Christianity throughout the Middle East. I've spoken to people in those countries who are fed up because their religion offers them no hope, no forgiveness, and no answers. Many of them are turning to faith in Christ, and we will learn more about our rare opportunity to reach them in the next chapter.

Chapter 11

TESTIMONY OF A FIRST-CENTURY TERRORIST

Imagine that you are sitting in your church singing songs when suddenly Osama bin Laden walks through the doors and sits down next to you. Why, he's even carrying a Bible! Would you move to a different part of the sanctuary, or would you put your arm around him and welcome him to the service? I would guess your reaction would be similar to how a man named Ananias of Damascus reacted when he found out God wanted him to talk to Saul of Tarsus.

Whom would you consider to be an "impossible case"—someone whom there would be no way this person could ever come to Christ? Everyone knows someone like that. In high school, I remember John Booth, a young man who was captain of the football team and a very intimidating person. After high school, I came to know Christ. At my ten-year high school reunion, I saw John Booth, and this same intimidating person wore a huge smile. I said, "John, how are you?"

"Great," he said. "I'm a Christian."

As we talked, I was thinking, *No way. John is the last person I would expect to become a Christian.* To me it had seemed impossible.

A couple was having dinner with a man who worked with a magician. The man said, "You know, from the audience's perspective, when an illusionist saws a woman in half and her body is separated, it looks impossible. But when you work in the business and it's explained to you, you discover it is very simple and not complicated at all."

At times, salvation looked impossible for the disciples, and in Matthew 19 they asked Jesus, "Who then can be saved?" (verse 25).

Jesus said, "With men this is impossible, but with God all things are possible" (Matthew 19:26).

This chapter addresses the opportunities we have to spread the gospel where God is at work in our world. It is the opposite of the last chapter, in which we examined the threat of radical Islam. God is working among the Muslim population in the Middle East in an unprecedented manner. Every hour, 666 Muslims convert to Christianity worldwide.[1] Every day that's sixteen thousand people who will give their lives to Christ. I've spoken to leaders and pastors of churches in Islamic countries who are telling me those same details. There is a real hunger and thirst for the truth of the gospel.

In this chapter, we're going to examine the life of Saul of Tarsus. In advance, please forgive me when I compare the great revered Apostle Paul to a modern-day terrorist. But in truth, before Saul of Tarsus was saved, he was a scoundrel. We're going to look at his life before he became the great missionary, letter writer, and doctrinal expositor of the New Testament. Before Saul was transformed, he was on a personal holy war to exterminate the Christian faith from that part of the world.

From Paul's life, I hope we will all begin to look at people differently from how we have viewed them in the past. No one, under any circumstances, is beyond the reach of the gospel.

In his first Law of Motion, Sir Isaac Newton stated that everything continues in a state of rest unless it is compelled to change by forces impressed upon it. When you apply that principle to Saul of Tarsus, you see that an outside Force impressed itself upon him and compelled him to change. As we consider this familiar story in Acts 9, I'm going to weave together stories, facts, and testimonials, not only about Saul's life, but also about those who have converted from radical Islam to faith in Jesus Christ.

Acts 9:1-2 tell us: "Then Saul, still breathing threats and murder against the disciples of the Lord, went to the high priest and asked letters from him to the synagogues of Damascus, so that if he found any who were of the Way, whether men or women, he might bring them bound to Jerusalem."

Saul was an angry man. The first mention of him in the Scriptures is in Acts 7:58, at the stoning of a young man named Stephen: "The witnesses [those who stoned Stephen] laid down their clothes at the feet of a young man named Saul" (words in brackets added). A few verses later, it says: "Saul was consenting unto his death" (Acts 8:1). Two verses later, in Acts 8:3: "Saul ... made havoc of the church." This word, *havoc*, is a strong word, implying the destruction of a wild boar that has trampled a garden or an army that has devastated a city. Saul was an angry man who was egging on the people who were stoning Stephen. He was saying, "Look, you really want to kill this man. Take off your coats so you can throw those rocks more easily. I'll watch your belongings for you."

Now in Acts 9:1, Saul was still breathing out threats and murder regarding believers, not only in Jerusalem, but Saul wanted to take his personal holy war against Christians to Damascus, 160 miles to the north. He was taking this murder show on the road.

This week I was reading about a young Muslim man named Mustafa, who grew up in Yemen and was introduced to radical Islam. As a teenager he developed a real hatred toward Christians; he even burned down a church in a village and stole from Christians under the banner of *jihad*,[2] or a holy war. He said, "I was filled with hatred for Christians. Christians have no rights." Later on God got ahold of Mustafa's life, and now he is a follower of Christ.

Saul of Tarsus, this angry young man, was determined to put out the light of Christianity in Jerusalem and then Damascus. One detail about Saul isn't given in this particular text. He was not only angry, but he was also wealthy. Saul's hometown was Tarsus, the most important commercial port in the province of Cilicia.[3] His parents sent him to an exclusive private school in Jerusalem to be mentored by a tutor named Gamaliel. (See Acts 22.) In our day, it would be the same as sending your son to an all-expenses-paid private school on the East Coast.

I mention Saul's wealthy background to point out another factor against the possibility he would ever make a decision to follow Christ. As Jesus said, "It's easier for a camel to go through the eye of a needle than for a rich man to get to heaven" (see Matthew 19:24). Often, wealthy people feel insulated from any sense of need because they feel they can always buy their way out of any problem.

Many young men involved in militant Islam come from wealthy families. For example, Osama bin Laden comes from a very wealthy Saudi family. Some of these young men growing up with wealth and time on their hands decide to use those resources for the cause of radical Islam.

Saul was not only from a wealthy family, but he was also very scholarly. I mentioned his private mentoring under Gamaliel in Jerusalem. This type of rigid upbringing forced Saul to memorize great portions of the Old Testament Law. He entered question-and-answer sessions. He was skilled in rhetoric and trained how to debate tough theological issues. Later on in Acts, Paul the Apostle, formerly Saul of Tarsus, stood on Mars Hill in Athens on the Aereopagus. As Paul spoke to the men of Athens, he quoted from memory two of their philosophers, Aerotus of Soli and Apemonedes, who had been dead for several hundred years. In today's world it would be like going to lunch with someone, and as you're talking to them, they begin to quote Shakespeare and C. S. Lewis from memory. You would think, *This guy's pretty smart!* But in 1 Corinthians 8, Paul wrote: "Knowledge puffs up." There are many scholarly people who feel insulated from their need for Christ. Scholars can often quickly and easily rationalize their spiritual condition and hide behind the smoke and mirrors of their own intellect.

I was reading of an Egyptian imam named Mark Gabriel[4] who has come to Christ. By the age of twelve, Gabriel had memorized the entire Koran so he could recite it from memory. In terms of length, the Koran is about the size of the New Testament. Just imagine being able to recite the entire New Testament at twelve years of age!

Saul of Tarsus was also very religious and devoted to his cause, as we learn from Philippians 3:5-6: "Concerning the law, [I was] a Pharisee ... concerning the righteousness which is in the law, [I was] blameless" (words in brackets added). As a Pharisee, Paul knew all of the major doctrinal precepts of the Old Testament. I've discovered that religious people are the hardest to convert to Christ because they hide behind their religion. They say, "I go to church," or, "Because I belong to some religious affiliation, I'm already good enough." Most religious people are among the most difficult to convince they're sinners in the need of a Savior. As a religious person, Saul of Tarsus justified his hatred. He felt his own religious convictions gave him permission to exterminate Christians.

Thirty years ago a young man named Daniel Shayesteh from Iran was caught up in a coup to overthrow the government, oust the Shah of Iran, and instill Islamic law through the Ayatollah Khomeini. Daniel said, "My background is radical Islam, and when you read the Koran it says that you must destroy other religions, Jews and Christians. You cannot expect them to value your values."[5]

In general, I have found Muslims to be devout, sincere, and dedicated people. This type of dedication certainly impressed a young Jewish man named David Gartenstein-Ross,[6] who was raised in Oregon by hippie parents. Gartenstein-Ross said, "It was a very liberal Jewish family. In our living room we had a picture of Jesus; in the backyard a statue of Buddha." It amounted to a mishmash of different ideologies. He said, "In my Muslim friends I saw their commitment and their dedication." It made such an impression on Gartenstein-Ross that he converted to Islam and joined a radical Islamic group. Today Gartenstein-Ross works for the FBI and is a born-again Christian.

A snapshot of the devotional life for most Muslims worldwide involves following the five pillars of Islam.[7] The first pillar is called the *Shahadah*, which is the declaration that no one is worthy of worship except God and Muhammad is the messenger of God. They believe that sentence is so holy it should only be uttered in Arabic when spoken in the ears of babies. Throughout life, it is recited, and then spoken in the ears of the elderly before they die. If non-Muslims can say those words and believe them in their heart, they are admitted to the Muslim community. The second pillar is the *Salah*, or the obligatory prayer five times a day facing Mecca with certain prescribed motions. The third pillar is the *Sawm*, or fasting for an entire month during Ramadan. Between sunrise and sunset of this month, Muslims don't eat, drink, or have sexual relations, so they will often get up early before sunrise to have a huge meal and then after sunset have another huge meal. The fourth pillar of Islam is *Zakah*, or the tithe, which emphasizes the principle that everything belongs to Allah. Each Muslim calculates his or her own *zakah* individually. This involves the annual payment of a fortieth of one's capital, excluding such items as primary residence, car, and professional tools. The fifth and final pillar is the *hajj*, or the pilgrimage to Mecca, which is required of every Muslim at least once during their lifetime.

However, even if a Muslim is religious, dedicated, devoted, and follows all five pillars religiously, they still have no guarantee they'll go to paradise. Judgment is based on the arbitrary will of God, which no one can predict. Even Mohammed was unsure that he'd go to Heaven; he even recorded that statement. If the founder of Islam, Mohammed himself, was unsure that he was going to go to paradise, how can any Muslim have assurance? The *single exception* is if any Muslim dies in service to Allah, no matter what else they have done, they will be guaranteed a place in paradise. Understanding this guarantee should help us see why certain worldwide events are taking place. Muslims believe if they die in service to Allah, then they are instantly admitted into paradise.

In the last chapter, I mentioned a theological principle called abrogation, which is necessary to understand the mentality of Muslims. *Abrogation* means annulling a former law by enacting a new law. If Allah makes a new statement, he can negate, nullify, or abrogate any previously made statements.[8] Allah is not bound by his revelations. He can say, "Yesterday I said that, and today I say this, and in the future I may say something totally different, but when I say something totally different, it can nullify everything I've said before." The importance of knowing which verses in the Koran abrogate or nullify other verses is almost a science.[9] One Muslim scholar explains: "God is absolutely free and unrestricted even in the realm of truth. He is free to abrogate truth of earlier revelations by subsequently revealed truths. He is free to judge the same act as good in one circumstance and evil in another according to the situation."[10] Doesn't this Islamic doctrine explain a great deal? It helps answer the question, "How can anyone claiming to follow any god perform those types of terrorist acts?" The god the Muslim serves changes his mind—and that concept is totally different from our understanding of God. Our God is consistent, and the Bible is the perfect source of revelation—absolute, inerrant, and consistent. We follow a Savior, Jesus, who said, "Heaven and earth may pass away but my word will never pass away." (See Matthew 5:18.) Or as the writer of Hebrews tells us: "Jesus Christ is the same yesterday, today, and forever" (13:8). And we know about God himself in Malachi 3:6, which says: "For I am the LORD, I do not change."

So, Saul of Tarsus was angry, wealthy, scholarly, religious, and now justifying what he was doing through his religion. But this "impossible case" turned into an incredible conversion. In Acts 9:3, Saul's agenda was interrupted: "As he journeyed he came near Damascus, and suddenly a light shone around him from heaven. Then he fell to the ground, and heard a voice ..."

When I read this verse, I thought, *Boy, God must really have wanted to save Saul, because He was willing to use such unusual circumstances to get his attention!* Isn't it good to know, when you think of loved ones or people who you thought were too far gone to be saved, that the Holy Spirit, the Hound of Heaven, is unrestricted and can do anything to get a person's attention? If you have a son or a daughter or a spouse who's so far from God that you believe, "There's no way of faith for this person," suddenly God *can* break through.

Earlier in this chapter, I mentioned Daniel Shayesteh from Iran who wanted to join the group to overthrow the Shah. Shayesteh eventually grew disillusioned with the whole idea of a coup. He defected from his political party and began his own. The leaders found out about his actions, arrested Shayesteh, beat him, took him over to Turkey, and threw him into prison.

He was alone and isolated in an Islamic prison, but one night he had a dream. In this dream, Shayesteh saw himself in his father's house back in Iran. He heard Jesus calling him to come out of the house. When he walked out of his father's house, Shayesteh turned around and watched the entire house crumble before him. Then he woke up. Soon after this dream and a series of circumstances, Shayesteh gave his life to the Lord. He said, "I think the supernatural intervention of God was a cue to cause me to wake up." After he gave his life to Christ, his wife and children saw his changed life and followed in his steps to make the decision to follow Jesus.

Notice the posture of Saul when Jesus asked him a question in Acts 9:4: "Then he fell to the ground ..." I love the thought of angry, wealthy, scholarly, religious, tough Saul on the ground when Jesus spoke to him. While Saul was out to silence the Christians, Christ came and spoke to him.

Jesus could have said many different things to Saul, but notice the graciousness of Jesus as He called him by his first name: "Saul, Saul" (verse 4). He didn't say, "Hey, idiot!" Instead Jesus asked, "Saul, Saul, why are you persecuting Me?" (verse 4). What a question!

Saul said, "Who are you, Lord?"

Jesus said, "I am Jesus, whom you are persecuting."

When I was in Israel working on a *kibbutz* (a farm), I met a man named Tony from England who had gone to Cambridge University. This very intelligent botanist was a verbal terrorist. Each day Tony would go out of his way to find me, because he knew that I and a few others believed in Jesus. He would mock Jesus to my face with his great vocabulary. To be honest, I thought, *There's no way this man will ever come to Christ.*

I returned home to America. A few months later my phone rang, and it was Tony, saying, "Hello, Skip?"

"Yes."

"I've given my life to Christ."

I said, "No way!" Yet his story was true. Tony had discovered a personal relationship with Jesus Christ.

Or consider the life of a young man named Timothy from Egypt, who was part of a mystical Islamic sect called the Sufri[11] sect. At the age of fourteen, Timothy became an evangelist and preached on the streets of Egypt, yet he wanted more intimacy with God. In a period of soul searching, Timothy said, "One night Christ appeared to me and said in a tender sweet voice, 'I love you.' I saw how obstinately I had resisted Him all these years. And I said to Him in tears, 'I love you, too. I know you. You are eternal forever and ever."[12] In an instant Timothy's life was transformed.

Look at Acts 9:5-6 and observe the process of change going on inside Saul's heart:

> He said, "Who are You, Lord?" Then the Lord said, "I am Jesus, whom you are persecuting. It is hard for you to kick against the goads." So he, trembling and astonished, said, "Lord, what do You want me to do?" Then the Lord said to him, "Arise and go into the city, and you will be told what you must do."

Saul was on a mission of terror, traveling to Damascus, when the Lord Jesus stopped him and Saul felt the prod of conviction. A goad is a prodding device.[13] Consider what had been happening to Saul. Everywhere he went, he met individual Jews who had converted to become followers of Jesus. Saul witnessed their changed lives, their joy, their peace, and their conviction. He watched as Stephen was stoned. As those rocks pelted Stephen's head and his blood gushed out, Saul held the coats of the men who were throwing the stones. The Bible says that Stephen's face shone like an angel when he looked up to Heaven and said, "Lord Jesus, don't lay this sin to their charge. Lord Jesus, receive my spirit."

The Pharisee from Tarsus had never seen this type of faith and graciousness, and the experience haunted him so that he probably couldn't sleep at night. Jesus asked him, "It's hard for you to kick against those goads, isn't it, Saul of Tarsus?"

A young man named Ahmed was once plagued with nightmares. Each night he'd wake up with the same nightmare about the coming judgment. Reading the Koran, Ahmed found no solace because it simply added to his fear of judgment. In secret, Ahmed found an Arabic Bible and sneaked the book into his room. When everyone was asleep, he would wake up, turn on the light, and start reading the Bible. Ahmed discovered Jesus Christ. He had known the name of Jesus from various references in the Koran, but in the Arabic Bible, he read about Jesus' life and the miracles He performed. One day in the mosque, Ahmed said in front of everyone to the imam, "Hey, why don't we respect Jesus Christ? He's mentioned in the Koran, and the Bible says He's a man of great miracles." Ahmed's words set off a firestorm. They kicked him out of the mosque, beat him up, called him an infidel, and said, "You must return to Islam." But Ahmed never looked back on his decision to follow Jesus Christ. Today young Ahmed is a Christian missionary, spreading the gospel message to Muslims.

To conclude this chapter, I want to return to the story of Saul and consider the reaction of a Christian believer named Ananias. Until this point, God had dealt with Saul supernaturally, without any human involvement, but now he chose to involve Ananias. Acts 9:10-11a says:

> Now there was a certain disciple at Damascus named Ananias; and to him the Lord said in a vision, "Ananias." And he said, "Here I am, Lord." So the Lord said to him, "Arise and go to the street called Straight."

Ananias had to be excited because he heard the unmistakable voice of God, but the voice told him to go to a street called Straight.

"I know right where that is; I live here," he would have said.

"Inquire ... for one called Saul of Tarsus, for behold, he is praying," the Lord said (Acts 9:11). Ananias heard dead silence, and then the voice of God continued:

"And in a vision he has seen a man named Ananias coming in and putting his hand on him, so that he might receive his sight." Then Ananias answered, "Lord, I have heard from many about this man, how much harm he has done to Your saints in Jerusalem. And here he has authority from the chief priests to bind all who call on Your name." (Acts 9:12-14)

The Lord said to him, "Go." Now notice what He said next:

"He [Saul] is a chosen vessel of Mine to bear My name before Gentiles, kings, and the children of Israel. For I will show him how many things he must suffer for My name's sake." (Acts 9:15-16)

How did Ananias respond when he heard Saul's name? Immediately he labeled Saul, saying, "He's an evil man who has done much harm to Your saints."

And Jesus said, "Yeah, that's what he *was*. Let me tell you what he is *now*. Saul is a chosen vessel of mine to bear my name to the world."

Let me ask you: What labels have you placed upon certain people you know or certain people in different parts of the world? Have you labeled them *impossible* or *unreachable*? Maybe you believe they've caused too much evil and harm that God doesn't even want to save them.

But the Lord says, "I want to take down that label and replace it by saying they are a chosen vessel of mine.

I can totally transform a life." We can never say about any person, "He'll never change." If you say those words, then you presume too much and believe too little. God can do anything with anyone. Saul's life screams that message to us. In fact, I would guess that some of you reading these words are the same individuals about whom people said, "No way." But you are now saying, "Yes, way!" Do you think some of those early Christians in Jerusalem and Damascus ever sat around and said, "Hey, wouldn't it be cool if Saul of Tarsus got saved?"

God took an impossible case and worked an incredible conversion. No one in any circumstance or any place is beyond God's touching them. Begin viewing people through a new lens, as a spiritual opportunity that may be disguised as impossibility. When you bring God into the equation, you'll start looking at people differently. Just think about it: There are 666 Muslims each hour coming to know Jesus. Tremendous opportunities await us if we follow the leading of our Lord!

Chapter 12

WHAT NOW?

Bernard Brown Jr. was the president of a group called Kennestone Health Management Care in Georgia. Years ago, while Brown was working at a local hospital, a patient accidentally spilled a glass of water. Because the water landed on the floor, the patient was afraid he might slip if he got up, so he called the nurse's aide and asked her to clean up the puddle.

A hospital policy had been recently enacted that said if it was a small puddle, then a nurse's aide should clean it up; if it was a large puddle, then housekeeping should clean it up. When the nurse's aide looked at the puddle, she determined it was a large puddle and called housekeeping. When the man from the housekeeping department looked at the puddle, he called it a small puddle. A full-blown argument broke out.

As they argued back and forth, the patient watched from his bed. Finally, the patient took his pitcher of water and dumped the whole thing on the floor, then said, "Now is the puddle big enough for you two to decide what to do?" The argument ended, and they both cleaned up the water.

What is our personal responsibility for homeland security? Throughout eleven chapters, we have looked at this topic. We have probed five different fronts to discover that our homes are under attack, our families are under attack, our souls are under constant barrage on a number of fronts, the Church is under attack, and finally our own national security is being assaulted.

While some situations may seem more threatening to you than others, how do we apply these truths on each front? To go back to the first chapter, how can we become like the children of Isaachar? First Chronicles 12:32 says: "The sons of Isaachar ... had understanding of the times, to know what Israel ought to do." These ordinary people were involved in an extraordinary battle, and God gave them wisdom. In the Book of Romans, Paul spent eleven chapters discussing what he called the mercies of God before he reached the text I wish to discuss: Romans 12.

Paul began the Book of Romans by declaring in chapters 1 through 3: "Everyone in the world is cut off and condemned by God because of sin. But everyone in the world can also be saved by God and justified." In chapter 4 Paul wrote that justification comes through an act of faith in Christ alone, just as Father Abraham believed God and it was counted to him for righteousness. Then in chapter 5 Paul said that because of our act of faith in Jesus, we now have access to God, the hope of Heaven. In chapters 6 through 8, Paul wrote that the act of justification leads to something even better: sanctification. God cleans us up and provides us with a power outside of ourselves, the Holy Spirit, to conquer sin and to help in our prayer life. Then in chapters 9 to 11, Paul declared that God would keep every promise made to the nation of Israel, as well as to the Gentile world. Each of those first eleven chapters of Romans tells of the mercies of God.

In chapter 12, Paul reached the heart of his message. Romans 12:1-2 says: "I beseech you therefore, brethren, by the mercies of God, that you present your bodies a living sacrifice, holy, acceptable to God, which is your reasonable service. And do not be conformed to this world, but be transformed by the renewing of your mind, that you may prove what is that good and acceptable and perfect will of God." Paul was saying, "God has done so much for you; *therefore* this is how you should respond."

We must have two responses to all that we have learned thus far. First, we must make the practical presentation of our bodies to God, saying, "Here I am, God. I'm yours, fully and totally." Our second response must be an inward transformation of our minds. We must change the way we think about the values around us. These two responses are critical to what we see in trends going around us. As college football coach Lou Holtz puts it, life is 10 percent what happens to you and 90 percent how you respond to what happens to you.

Our first response is a practical presentation, an emphasis on our lifestyles. Paul wrote: "Present your bodies a living sacrifice" (Romans 12:1). The word *present* is a technical word that refers to the time in Leviticus when the priest offered a sacrifice on the altar as atonement for the sins of the nation. Just as the priest presented the animal to God on behalf of the nation, we are to present our bodies to God as a living sacrifice.

Now let's focus on the word *living*. This is the difference from the Old Testament sacrifices—because the animal sacrifices were dead. The priest killed the animal, bled the animal out, and sometimes used fire to consume the animal. The animal was once and for all given over to God. But Paul wrote: "Brethren, make a living sacrifice." That's a little tougher, because living sacrifices have a tendency to squirm off the altar. We say something like, "God, I'm giving you my life. Well, on second thought, I'd like that little piece for myself just for another few days, and then I'll give it right back to you." No, when you make yourself a living sacrifice, you must undergo a total change in lifestyle.

Notice that Romans 12:1 says, we should "present [our] bodies." Why would God want our bodies? Sometimes I hear Christians talk as though the body is evil and God doesn't really care about it. They think God only cares about the heart. But God *does care* about our bodies. Do you know why? If our bodies are yielded to God, they become a base of operations for the work of the Holy Spirit. Your body is *Command Central* for the Holy Spirit to work in your neighborhood, in your job, or in your classroom. The Holy Spirit can function from this base of operations; this is why the Bible calls our bodies the temple of the Holy Spirit.

The Bible is filled with wonderful examples of bodies yielded over to God. Consider the womb of Sarah, who was barren and elderly. Yet she yielded her body over to God even though she wasn't too excited about doing it, and she became a wonderful receptacle for the son of promise, a boy, Isaac. Or I think about Moses' mouth, which was yielded over to God. About himself, Moses said: "God, I can't speak. I'm a man of uncircumcised speech." But when he yielded his body over to God, Moses' mouth became a powerful instrument; it spoke to Pharaoh and uttered the Law to the nation of Israel. Or think about David's hands. As a shepherd boy, David yielded those hands over to God. When David put a sling and a stone in those hands and yielded his body to God, he vanquished Goliath. I think of the feet of the Apostle Paul, who carried the gospel from Jerusalem to Judea, to Samaria, and to the uttermost parts of the Earth. In truth, God wants to touch the world through you and me, and so we present our bodies for His service.

Notice something else in Romans 12:1. Paul concluded this verse by saying, "Which is your reasonable service." This word *reasonable* is the Greek word *logicos*, from which we get the word *logical*. You must make a rational choice. But it makes sense if you think about all God has done in the past, all of the mercies of God, the way He's provided a way for you to be saved, and the way He's provided for you to have peace in times of suffering. It is logical that you would want to present your body to Him! You should want to commit your life to God because God has given you all of the resources necessary for life and godliness.

Let's think through the list of the five topics from the last eleven chapters and see if we're presenting ourselves to God.

First, is your eternal future secure? In your own heart and mind, have you presented yourself to God in this area? If you recall, in one of the first chapters, we looked at the Leaning Tower of Pisa, which is leaning and one day will fall. Why? Because the tower was built on a poor foundation. What type of foundation is your life built on? Is it secure?

Some people have a false sense of security because they are running through life wrongly believing they are Heaven-bound when they are not. Jesus issued a warning when He said: "Not everyone who says to Me, 'Lord, Lord,' shall enter the kingdom of heaven" (Matthew 7:21). Here's the bottom line when people say, "Oh, now you've got religion": If your religion hasn't changed you, then it's time for you to change your religion. Better yet, you need to secure a solid relationship with God through Christ alone. Some people have a false sense of security, and others have a flimsy sense of security, which means they're saved but every day they wake up wondering about it. They're always fluctuating and never certain about their eternal security. We need to believe the truth of 1 John 5:13, which says: "These things I have written to you who believe in the name of the Son of God, that you may know that you have eternal life." In chapter 3, I compared a person who is secure in their salvation to a ticketed, confirmed passenger, rather than a person on standby. If you've got your confirmed ticket, then you can read a newspaper, grab a meal, talk to your friends, or take a nap. But if you're on standby, you pace back and forth around the desk, hoping they'll call your name. You dare not leave the gate area. The big difference between the two passengers is confidence.

To emphasize this aspect in a different manner, my friend, pastor and teacher Dr. David Jeremiah, said, "We live in some very interesting days which have more challenges for us as Christ-followers than any generation that's ever lived on the face of this earth. Many times as they look around, Christians can get discouraged because it seems like in every direction there are issues and problems—with the economy, with the war, with the culture, with our families and with our finances. Where do we go to find the answers? The ultimate answer is in the Bible itself. But specifically, how do we live in these days? I've been learning something that I think has profound implications for each of us. We need to understand God has placed each of us, right now and here in this generation. We could have been born in any other time but God chose to place us here and this is our calling. We need to embrace that calling and understand God has placed us lights in the darkness and salt in the midst of decay. With all of our hearts, we need to find out what God wants us to do and what part he wants us to play. When we do that, we'll begin to discover the joy of being used by the Almighty to make a difference in a world that is in deep trouble. Because we know the last chapter, we know God has an ultimate plan and what a thrill to be included in that plan."

Indeed, I agree with Dr. Jeremiah that it's a thrill, so what do we do? When we know that our lives are on a secure foundation, then we must let it show. If we know it, then it will show. If we don't know about our salvation, then that will also show.

Second, is your family secure? Earlier in this book, we studied David and his relationship with his son Absalom. The home life of King David was basically Dysfunction Junction. As a passive father, David let his children run rampant, and he lost the moral high ground and couldn't speak any longer into his son's life. The family is the basic core of any culture: If the culture has strong families, then the society will be strong. But if the culture has weak families, then the society will be weak. Our culture has powerful forces at work to undermine our families. It is not just media, music, or film eroding our family structure, but sometimes it is parents themselves. Dr. James Dobson said: "The western world stands at a great crossroads in its history. It is my opinion that our very survival as a people will depend on the presence or absence of masculine leadership within the home. Over the past thirty years, the rise in violent crime parallels the rise in families abandoned by fathers. This is very critical."

John Fuller is the cohost of the *Focus on the Family* radio broadcast with Dr. James Dobson. I asked John to share a few words for this book. He said: "At *Focus on the Family* we believe the family is foundational to society, and without a doubt there are a lot of external pressures on families such as media coming into the home, distorting values, and many factors in the educational system. Certainly children are developing patterns that are not healthy for families. Also, moms and dads have internal things going on where sometimes they are too busy and preoccupied to pay much attention to the children and their needs. Between the external and the internal challenges coming at families, there's no doubt families are probably under the most stress and strain that they have been forever, at least in this culture. I've observed fathers are very good at setting goals at work and have no problem throwing all their emotional energies into their work. Then when these fathers go home spent, they pretty much check out from the role God has given them as a father to their children. I feel bad for dads who are missing it, by pouring a hundred percent into the work world and then going home with nothing. The truth of the matter is, most of us are replaceable at work but in our God-given role in family, we're irreplaceable.

"When I speak to dads, I encourage them to make the time, the energy, and some plans to be intentional in their parenting with their children. If you don't pour into the child's life, then the culture will, and what the culture gives is probably antithetical to your value system and in the long term going to harm that child. Speak into your child's life. We've got to be ready and willing when our children want to talk, and we have to be far more intentional than our natural tendency. I would encourage you to set goals for your children's spiritual milestones and help them navigate life. Then, when they leave the home, your children will be ready to be fruitful, productive citizens, and more importantly, men and women of God."

I want to pick up on John's use of the phrase "men and women of God" combined with his emphasis on intentional parenting. This type of intentional parenting begins with a response like Joshua gave as the leader of not only the nation of Israel, but his home. He said to the people: "As for me and my house, we will serve the LORD" (Joshua 24:15). Parents, think of yourselves as partners with God in discipling your children.

Third, is your home secure? Remember that Nehemiah wept over the city of Jerusalem when he heard that the gates were burned with fire and that the walls were broken down. Now, as the gatekeeper to your own soul and as gatekeepers to the souls of your children and of your family, what are you letting in the gates? What are you allowing your eyes to see and your ears to hear? While you may have wonderful homes and fancy security systems, what's going into those little holes called the Internet and cable television? What good is it to build up the walls of our lives through Bible study, prayer, and fellowship, when we're letting enemies in through the gates? As Proverbs 25:28 declares: "Whoever has no rule over his own spirit is like a city broken down, without walls." If you exercise no self-control, you are an easy victim.

My friend and Bible teacher Raul Ries comments about computers in the home: "I wanted to speak about the homeland security problem. Computers are both a good thing and a bad thing. I have counseled many men who have computers in their homes, and they are going to those websites that destroy men's character and their marriage because they are into pornography. There is a real bad situation where men have literally lost hope for their wives and their children and begun to do things that are not biblical. The only way you can be held back from pornography is to wash your minds with the Word of God. I encourage you to read the Bible and pray every day and then also to confess and repent of your sins and stay away from those websites on your computer. If you turn on the television, do not to go to those channels, or limit your television to regular public viewing. Spiritually, you've got to get rid of the sin. To get rid of the sin, you have to first repent of your sins, and second, as you repent, do not keep the same problem before you. And the only way is to never go back to reading or watching or listening to anything that is not decent and in order according to the Word of God. Pornography, especially, is killing and destroying our country, our nation, and marriages. Yes, victory is possible, but it's up to a person to submit, yield himself to the Holy Spirit, surrender his life, truly repent, and never go back to that sin or it will blind you and kill him." The only way for what Raul has said to make sense is for us to present our bodies completely to God in this area.

Fourth, is your church secure? To answer this question, we studied Luke 21, in which Jesus promised anyone who follows Him will not have an easy road. When you become a believer and go to church, it is not going to be a walk in the park. Instead, Jesus told us that the religious establishment is going to hate us. Some of us know exactly what it is to be persecuted by our religious families and friends. We gave our lives to Christ, but our old friends like our old selves better than our new selves.

Jesus also said the secular world will hate us. In His words, we will be brought before kings and rulers. He said we'd be hated by our families, betrayed by our parents and brothers, relatives and friends. Christians are persecuted around the world—it's estimated that one in every two hundred Christians can expect to be martyred in his or her lifetime. This kind of hatred is on the increase, not just overseas but also on our own shores.

Also in these pages, we've examined a much greater threat: some of the trends inside the Church and the battle over truth. The Apostle Paul said, "The time will come when they will not endure sound doctrine" (2 Timothy 4:3). A disturbing trend falls under the banner of the Emerging

Church, a sort of spiritual terrorism and a subtle sabotage of the truth. In fact, the leaders of this movement are saying, "It's not even possible for you to know what truth really is." Brian McLaren, one of the spokespersons for the Emerging Church, said, "I don't know if anyone has ever gotten the Gospel right." This "anyone" would include Paul, Peter, and John and to say they didn't get the gospel right is disturbing.

I've asked Josh McDowell to provide a few words about this topic, especially what he calls the Last Christian Generation. Josh said: "I am thankful you're taking time to look at homeland security. We need to realize that in Jesus Christ, we can have a phenomenal peace right in the midst of terror. When I wrote *The Last Christian Generation*, it was probably the hardest book I ever had to start on a topic, and I didn't want to write it but I felt I had to. It's more like a twenty-first-century Christian manifesto. As I have worked with young people now for forty-seven years—traveling, speaking, writing, interacting—I have concluded this generation of young people in general is not a Christian generation, not by what they believe nor how they behave. The last Christian generation is not our young people today, it's the parents, and it hurts to say that. I couldn't have written the first half of my book unless I believed there were positive, biblically based, culturally relevant answers, one family at a time."

I want to pick up on Josh's phrase "culturally relevant answers." In this postmodern era, even with the Emerging Church saying there are only mysteries and no answers, when you give culturally relevant answers, it makes a huge difference. Postmodernism is creating a whole generation of disillusioned people who are groping for the truth. Our solution isn't to drag the Gospel down to their level but to lift people up to the level of the truth as we stand up for it. I want you to be personally discerning when it comes to what is true and what is not true, to have a good filtering system.

Fifth, are you telling others how to be secure? Are you seeing the opportunities in our world? We examined Islam in several chapters of this book. Think about it: Twenty percent of the world's population is Muslim, which is one out of every five people on the planet, or 1.3 billion people who would love to see the worldwide spread of Islam. In the United States a new mosque opens every week. Radical Islam is comprised of a significant number of people who want to see the Great Satan, or the United States, utterly destroyed, along with the Little Satan, or Israel. Did you know that Osama bin Laden refers to 9/11 as "that blessed Tuesday, September 11th"? For that man and some of these radicals, September 11, 2001, was a threshold moment.

But what about the opportunity? The conversion of Saul of Tarsus proves that no one is beyond the reach of the gospel. Saul was a first-century terrorist, and Jesus Christ still got ahold of his life. At that time, people thought, *No way will Saul ever become a believer*, yet it happened. All over the Islamic world, every day thousands upon thousands are coming to Christ. I have asked Joel C. Rosenberg and Kamal Saleem[1] to tell us briefly what's happening in that part of the world.

Joel Rosenberg said: "One of the things people don't realize, even among evangelical Christians, is how powerfully God is moving right now in the Middle East, and the Church is growing by leaps and bounds. In the Middle East, more Muslims are coming to faith in Jesus Christ today than at any other time in the history of the world. Of course, Jesus did say, 'I will build my church and the gates of hell will not prevail against it.' I'm not sure Christians really believed that when it came to the Muslim world for centuries and centuries and centuries. Now we are seeing absolute miracles going on in the epicenter."

Kamal Saleem added: "Muslims are coming to Christ all over the Middle East today. God is taking radical Muslims who are about to kill innocent people and saying, 'Rise up; you are my warrior.'"

Joel Rosenberg continued:

Back in the early 1990s, there was a series of assassinations of Iranian Christian leaders, and as those began to unfold, a lot of Christian ministries told their leadership, "You need to get out of the country at least for a while; it's not safe." And so phone calls started moving around, and these guys from the Iranian Bible Society got the call where they were told, "You've got to get out of the country as fast as you can." Because of what they do, this Bible Society leader grabbed a bunch of boxes of Bibles in the Iranian language of Farsi,[2] put them in the backseat of his car, and as fast as they could, began driving up into the mountains. As they drove on the road, a rainstorm began and got harder and harder as they drove those winding mountain roads, which are very narrow, and then suddenly their steering wheel locks. By God's grace, the car stopped right on the edge of the cliff. Suddenly on the car window, they heard a knock, which startled them, and a man's face appeared in their window. The man said, "Do you have books?"

Puzzled, they said, "What are you talking about?"

The man continued, "Did you see that village at the top of that hill? That's where I live, and about a week ago I had a vision where Jesus told me, 'Go down the mountain and wait by the side of the road, and someone will bring you my book that will tell you how to live.'"

As the man told this story, these two men from the Iranian Bible Society thought, *Okay, I guess that's why we're here.* The men got out of their car, pulled out the Bibles, and began to give them to the man, who began to weep. He took the Bibles, put them underneath his coat, and hiked back up the mountain. When these men turned their car back on, the steering wheel worked, and they drove out of the country.

That story is awesome and a true example of what God is doing today in the Middle East. Remember the story of Saul of Tarsus in the Book of Acts. The man named Ananias had labeled Saul of Tarsus, saying to God, "I have heard how many evil things he has done to harm your people." What labels have we placed on people's lives that the Lord would want us to take down? He wants to transform those people and make them believers in Jesus Christ. We must take the practical step of saying, "Here I am, Lord. Here is my body, which is devoted to you."

Finally, we must have an inward transformation. Romans 12:2 says: "And do not be conformed to this world, but be transformed by the renewing of your mind, that you may prove what is that good and acceptable and perfect will of God." God is calling you to nonconformity, so do not conform to this world. I love the Phillips' translation of Romans 12:2: "Don't let the world squeeze you into its own mold." One of our greatest fears is to be rejected by our peers and to somehow be different from others. But as a result, we conform to what the world thinks.

Years ago a group of scientists put caterpillars on top of a clay pot as an interesting experiment. They put the caterpillars head to tail, head to tail, all the way around, to create a solid ring of caterpillars around the clay pot. Then they watched as the caterpillars marched around and around. They marched not for just an hour or one day or a second day. They marched around all week until they died of starvation and exhaustion. Not one caterpillar broke away from the group to get nourishment, for inside the pot was a plant, or food for caterpillars. Instead, each caterpillar followed another caterpillar until each one died. Our world acts just like those processional caterpillars.

As believers in Jesus Christ, we are not to be conformed to the world, but we are to be transformed. Our thinking is to be renewed: "[But you] be transformed by the renewing of your mind" (Romans 12:2; words in brackets added).

Your mind matters to God. Jesus said you are to love the Lord your God with all of your heart, mind, soul, and strength (see Matthew 22:37). We are conforming to one of two value systems: the value system of God and His Word or the value system of this world. We should think deeply about these issues through the lens of the Bible, which shapes our thinking so that we think God's thoughts. As James Montgomery Boice wrote:

> People aren't thinking anymore. Brain cells are seriously underexercised. *Contemplation* has become an old-fashioned word with little place in our fast-paced, high-tech world. For thinking, we have substituted entertainment. The substitution has been so effective that many of us believe that entertainment actually makes us think. We think of ourselves as being the best-informed generation in history because

of television. Television is not informing us. It's entertaining us and there is a difference.

I encourage you to break away from the crowd, dare to be different, and think differently. If you think biblically, I'll guarantee you will be thinking differently from the rest of the crowd. Think differently about your need for a spiritual foundation. Think differently about your need to nurture your family. Think differently about securing your soul and your home from soul thieves. Think differently about securing the Church and standing up for the truth. And let's not argue over petty little things like, "Is that a big puddle or a little puddle?" Instead, let's go get a towel and clean it up together.

ENDNOTES

CHAPTER 1

1   http://www.crosswalk.com/news/religiontoday/11596965/.

2   http://www.utne.com/1996-09-01/Politics/LifeWithoutFather.aspx?page=2.

3   http://www.jihadwatch.org/2007/06/56-of-atheists-and-agnostics-think-radical-christianity-is-just-as-threatening-in-america-as-radical.html.

4   http://en.wikiquote.org/wiki/Edmund_Burke.

CHAPTER 4

1   http://www.standupforkids.org.

2   http://www.e-gracenotes.org/article.php?id=2050.

3   http://www.standupforkids.org.

CHAPTER 5

1   *USA Today*, October 9, 2003, p. D1.

CHAPTER 6

1   *Back to the Bible Today*, Summer 1990, p. 5.

2   http://www.sermoncentral.com/sermon.asp?SermonID=54514.

3   Http://findarticles.com/p/articles/mi_m2372/is_4_38/
     ai_84866951/.

4   *Internet Filter Review*, 2004.

CHAPTER 7

1   James Hefley and Marti Hefley, *By Their Blood: Christian
     Martyrs from the Twentieth Century and Beyond*, Baker
     Books, a division of Baker Book House Company, P.O. Box
     6287, Grand Rapids, MI 49516-6287, Copyright 1979, 1996.

2   http://en.wikipedia.org/wiki/Onward_Christian_Soldiers.

3   http://sermonillustrations.com/a-z/o/onward_christian_
     soldiers.htm.

CHAPTER 8

1   http://en.wikipedia.org/wiki/Athanasius_of_Alexandria.

2   http://www.creeds.net/ancient/nicene.htm.

3   http://www.quotationspage.com/quote/23633/html.

4   http://www.citynewsstand.com/TopTen.htm.

5   http://www.sermonillustrations.com/a-z/t/truth.htm.

6   Revelation 2:14.

7   http://www2.wcc-coe.org/pressreleasesen.nef/index/Feat-08-
     04.html.

8   http://www.religion-online.org/showarticle.asp?title=770.

9   http://en.wikipedia.org/wiki/Chung_Hyun_Kyung.

10   http://books.google.com/books?id=J-NKaygPPBMC&pg=
     PA24&lpg=PA24&dq=my+bowel+is+a+Shamanist+bowel
     &source=web&ots=E0ZbD6ELdF&sig=VvzqgHbQw98Pj
     7t_y8v4GEVL8Y8&hl=en.

11   http://www.carols.org.uk/ba27-joy-to-the-world.htm.

12   http://bible.crosswalk.com/Lexicons/Greek/grk.
     cgi?number=1319.

13   http://www.lgmarshall.org/Reformed/boice_knowing.html.

14   http://www.answersingenesis.org/articles/am/v2/n4/
     emerging-church.

15   http://theoblogy.blogspot.com/2007/06/jerry-falwell.html.

16 http://www.angelfire.com/f15/hleewhite/ecc1chasingthewind.
   htm.

CHAPTER 9

1 http://www.ntwords.com/preach5.htm.
2 http://www.gracereformedbaptist.ca/site/recreading.asp?sec_
   id=140000343.
3 http://www.hcs.harvard.edu/~gsascf/shield.html
4 http://www.bnltimes.com/content/view/1516/112/.

Chapter 10
1 http://www.amconmag.com/01_13_03/borchgrave7.htm.
2 http://www.amconmag.com/article/2003/jan/13/00029/.
3 http://www.freerepublic.com/focus/news/803200/posts.
4 http://www.encyclopedia.com/doc/1O142-onager.html.
5 http://en.wikipedia.org/wiki/Ibn_Ishaq.
6 http://en.wikipedia.org/wiki/Brigitte_Gabriel.
7 http://www.amazon.com/Because-They-Hate-Survivor-
   Islamic/dp/0312358377.
8 http://www.milnet.com/Gabriel-Transcript.html.
9 http://transcripts.cnn.com/TRANSCRIPTS/0612/21/gb.01.
   html.
10 http://www.americanthinker.com/2005/01/allahs_special_
   little_apes_and.html.

CHAPTER 11

1 http://mensnewsdaily.com/2006/12/31/over-a-million-
   muslim-converts-to-christianity/.
2 http://en.wikipedia.org/wiki/Jihad.
3 http://www.sacred-destinations.com/turkey/tarsus.htm.
4 http://www.markagabriel.org/index.php?option=com_content
   &task=view&id=27&Itemid=49.
5 http://www.journalgazette.net/apps/pbcs.dll/
   article?AID=/20070929/FEAT/709290381.

6   http://www.weeklystandard.com/Content/Public/
    Articles/000/000/012/532dxbll.asp.

7   http://www.islam101.com/dawah/pillars.html.

8   http://shadhilitariqa.com/site/index.php?option=com_
    content&task=view&id=37.

9   http://www.jihadwatch.org/archives/013367.php.

10 http://www.answering-islam.org/Authors/Schlorff/schlorffl_f.
    html.

11 http://answers.yahoo.com/question/index?qid=200711291847
    26AAIFXAd.

12 http://tinyurl.com/66anwb.

13 http://www.merriam-webster.com/dictionary/goad.

CHAPTER 12

1   http://www.wwj.org.nz/gfactsevang.php.

2   http://www.farsinet.com/farsi/.